THE SWEDISH
SMÖRGÅSBORD

ALL THE ORIGINAL RECIPES IN MODERN STYLE
RECIPES: GERT KLÖTZKE AND NICLAS WAHLSTRÖM
TEXTS: DONALD BOSTRÖM   PHOTOGRAPHY: PER-ERIK BERGLUND

BOKFÖRLAGET MAX STRÖM

Index

ROUND 1

ROUND 2

ROUND 3

ROUND 4

ROUND 5   ROUND 6   ROUND 7   ROUND 8

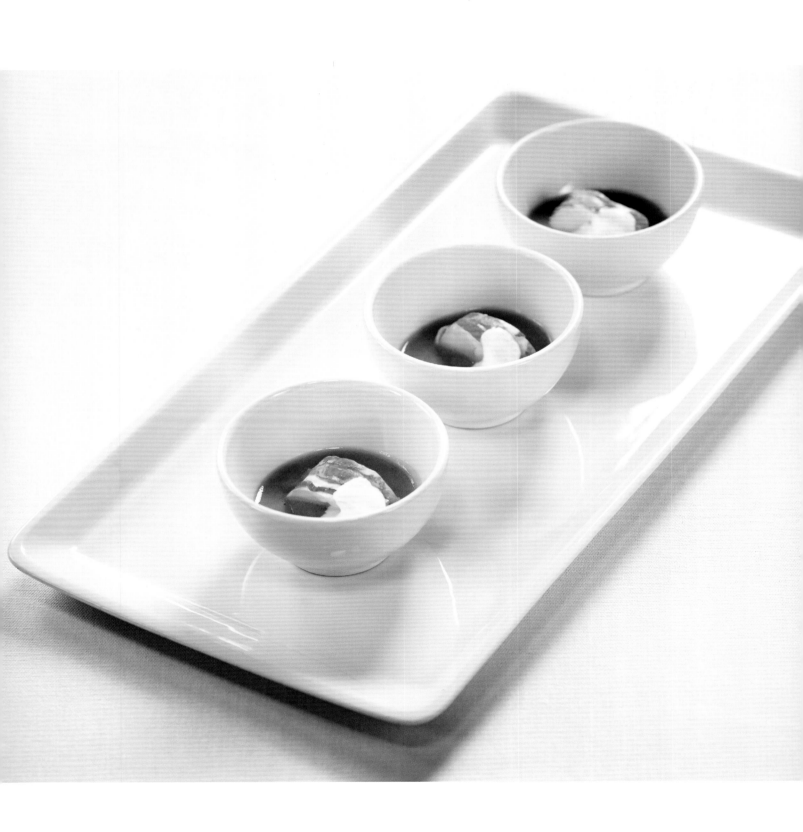

We let the food do its own talking

The smörgåsbord must be a pleasure for all the senses. In this book we have tried to present exciting new taste sensations but without losing "sight" of the familiar Swedish flavours. In our recipes the food speaks for itself, without any superfluous accretions. Our aim is for everyone to feel at home and for the craftsmanship of the food to live on. At the same time we have been mindful of the aesthetic aspect, for example by having the dishes in the eight rounds of the smörgåsbord served in little pieces. For the smörgåsbord must also be a feast for the eye.

   All the time our point of departure has been the thoughts of Tore Wretman as he set about renewing the smörgåsbord inherited from the 19th century. But adding one more round consisting entirely of vegetables, we have sought to modernise things in our way. The result: a smörgåsbord to suit all tastes, occasions and generations.
Enjoy!

From brännvinsbord to smörgåsbord

Sweden's world-famous smörgåsbord began life in the 16th century as a drinks table, a *brännvinsbord*, set with small goodies to keep the wolf from the door till dinner was served.

Invited guests arriving by horse and carriage would step into the parlour and help themselves to the spirits and the cold dishes. Standing, or seated plate-on-knee, they might talk for hours until the last guests had arrived and the meal proper could begin. Today the smörgåsbord is a worldwide success, but the road from *brännvinsbord* to smörgåsbord has been both long and devious.

For several centuries the smörgåsbord was an institution among the well-to-do, but it has also had its detractors. It was not until Tore Wretman, that legendary maître de cuisine, addressed the subject in the middle of the last century that the smörgåsbord became a national institution in Sweden. Today it has both refinement and the common touch and, above all, is quintessentially Swedish.

The 16th century brännvinsbord consisted of bread and butter, cheese, fish, meat and snaps and was always served cold, straight from the larder, often with local and seasonal variations.

Simultaneously with Gustav Vasa, Tycho Brahe, Martin Luther and the Reformation, Sweden was afflicted by war, famine and pestilence. Many farmsteads up and down the country were so badly hit that they were granted tax exemption. During those turbulent times a new kind of table – the *brännvinsbord* – evolved which included several dishes.

Having several dishes at once was a perfectly natural arrangement, not least in Swedish agrarian society, where nothing was wasted. At slaughtering time, chops and filets were not the only products taken care of. The animal's head was turned into brawn and its blood was literally used to the last drop. This resulted in a number and variety of dishes to put on the table. Sweden was not alone in this practice of serving several small dishes. Russia has a counterpart called *zakuski*, and the luxurious gorging of the Romans evolved into an Italian tradition of small dishes which in turn is presumed to have spawned the tapas of Spain. Denmark has had *det kolde bord* since the 16th century, often associated with weddings and major festive occasions and having snaps and pork as its mainstay. In the Eastern Mediterranean and Lebanon they call it *meze*. Sweden's *brännvinsbord* changed very little for a number of centuries, but then in the 19th century came a technical invention which changed the course of culinary history, namely the iron stove. The step from an open fire to hotplates and oven dramatically transformed the art of cooking and spurred the development of the smörgåsbord. With open fires, cooking had mostly meant boiling. The iron stove had plates and an oven, which meant that food could now be fried, roasted or baked and cooked in completely new ways. The smörgåsbord has never looked back since.

The meatball, a classic of the smörgåsbord, was made possible by the introduction of the mincer, during the mid-19th century. Meat could now be minced instead of just scraped into little pieces. For centuries, food had been dried, salted down, pickled and marinated. Now, with the stove and the mincer, the foundations were laid of our classical Swedish flavours and the Swedish smörgåsbord.

An important factor in the transition from *brännvinsbord* to classical smörgåsbord was a growth in the number of dishes on the table and the introduction of hot ones. Towards the end of the 19th century, more genteel eating establishments appeared on the Swedish scene. Luxury restaurants, hostelries and railway restaurants provided the smörgåsbord, which in this way became familiar to growing numbers of people. The smörgåsbord blossomed forth in its full splendour towards the end of the 19th century, but it also had its detractors. Young people thought it was strictly for wealthy, fat old men.

But the smörgåsbord survived the assaults of the knuts (*grilljanne* in Swedish), very much due to its becoming established as a Christmas table. 1919 is a historic year for the smörgåsbord. That year, for the first time ever, the Swedish Academy mentioned the word *julbord* (Christmas table), and the smörgåsbord had arrived, once and for all. In 1912, the year of the Stockholm Olympics, restaurants went, so to speak, the whole hog, offering the smörgåsbord as main course "with nothing to follow".

The smörgåsbord hit the international scene at the New York World's Fair in 1939, when it was presented in the Swedish pavilion and became one of two Swedish words to have been globally exported, the other one being *ombudsman*.

It was Tore Wretman who effectively introduced the smörgåsbord into Sweden's welfare state. From his base at the Operakällaren restaurant he made it internationally renowned. Tore Wretman's inspiration came from France, and for the first time the smörgåsbord was now structured. Whereas previously the different dishes had been put out more or less at random, Tore Wretman took the view that the food should be relished in a particular sequence, and accordingly he created five rounds.

The first round contained herring, Baltic herring and cheese, while other fish like salmon and eel came in the second round. The third round contained cold meats like liver paste and brawn, while the fourth featured small hot dishes like meatballs and Jansson's Temptation. The fifth and last round consisted of desserts like Maltese rice, apple tart, punch tart and fruit salad.

Following on from where Tore Wretman left off, Gert Klötzke and Niclas Wahlström are carefully modernising the classic Swedish smörgåsbord with an additional three new rounds and new recipes. The fifth round, which was dessert, now becomes the green round, with vegetarian dishes. The sixth round is devoted entirely to cheese and the desserts, now with confectionery added, do not come until the seventh. The eighth and final round consists of coffee, cakes and biscuits.

Compose your rounds carefully, don't mix the flavours, and allow yourself plenty of time to savour and enjoy.

Food and snaps in harmony

How is harmony created between the food we eat and the drink served with it? The idea is for the combination of food and drink to heighten the total experience of the moment at the table. Harmony of flavour depends on the drink not drowning the flavours of the food but bringing them out, and vice versa.

Taste is a personal thing – you are the only one who can decide what you like eating and drinking. There is no right or wrong of taste to which the personal experience of taste is subordinate, but the theory of taste formulated by Tim Hanni in the USA at the beginning of the 1990s has proved to work with the overwhelming majority of people. He starts with the five basic tastes which are statistically verifiable, at least sufficiently to convey a credible picture of how tastes function in different combinations.

The five basic tastes we can distinguish are sweet, sour, salt, bitter and umami. Umami is a relative newcomer in this connection, and its recognition as a "genuine" basic taste remains a moot point. The basic tastes are captured at different points in the mouth and on the tongue. Sweetness is best felt on the tip of the tongue, salt on the sides at the front of the tongue, sourness further back along the sides of the tongue and bitterness at the very rear. The hundreds of other aromas which we experience as taste are actually fragrances, as is confirmed by the classic test of holding one's nose while sampling a mixture of sugar and cinnamon. When we cannot smell the fragrance, the basic sweet taste is all we perceive of the mixture. If on the other hand we let go of our noses, the cinnamon aroma becomes clearly noticeable.

When combining food and drink one has to take into account, not only the basic tastes but also the flavour strength and spiciness of the food. Put simply, the rule is mild drinks with mild food and tasty drinks with tasty food, so that there will be no risk of either of them getting the upper hand.

- Sweetness in food reduces the experience of sweetness in drink.
- Salt reduces all other taste sensations, making the sweet less sweet, the astringent less astringent. Salt neutralises the bitter and sour.
- Sourness is the antithesis of sweetness, and the two are often balanced in food and drink. Sourness in food intensifies the experience of sweetness in drink.
- Bitterness accentuates bitterness and pungency.
- Umami, quite tellingly, is Japanese for "delicate" or "tasty", it is semi-sweet and is present, for example, in crab and king scallop, certain vegetables and fungi. Umami heightens sensitivity to bitterness, while salinity softens the effect of umami.

The typical Swedish tastes which we find on the smörgåsbord are sweet-and-sour and three of our basic tastes: sweet, sour and salt. The historical roots of our Swedish tastes are easy to see: before the refrigerator was invented, people pickled, marinated, salted and dried food to make it more durable. Swedish pickling – *gravning* – it will be remembered, is done with salt and sugar, and herring is pickled in sour distilled vinegar (*ättika*). These are typically Swedish, or rather, typically Nordic tastes.

Snaps

Spiced snaps occupies a strong position on the smörgåsbord. It came originally from the monasteries of Europe, as a medicine for the Black Death, among other things, in the 14th century. Gradually people began drinking it for its flavour, together with pickled, marinated, salted and dried food.

One reason for the popularity of spiced snaps at the smörgåsbord is that it does not contain any of the basic tastes sour, salt or sweet, thus eliminating the risk of taste collisions and giving snaps a wide range of applications – unlike wine, for example. In addition, the caraway, dill, aniseed, fennel and coriander flavouring of snaps makes for a brilliant partnership with the flavourings of the smörgåsbord. Moreover, the alcohol has taste-reinforcing properties which release the aromas in the same way as fat and sugar used in cooking. And it is actually true that spirits break down fats, which comes in handy when negotiating the eight rounds of the smörgåsbord. Both the snaps in itself and its spices facilitate digestion of these groaning buffets.

Considerations of taste are in fact the very reason why we have chosen to gear this book to the eight rounds of the smörgåsbord. From round one with its herring, Baltic herring and eggs, to round eight with its coffee, biscuits and confectionery. One round is followed by the next, piloting the tastes onwards without any fear of collisions.

Snaps hints for the eight rounds of the smörgåsbord

Snaps has its appointed place on the smörgåsbord. Its lack of basic flavours makes it easy to combine with the various dishes. For good combinations of flavours, be guided by the respective pungencies of the snaps and what you are eating. To do justice, for example, to a mild, creamy *strömming* (Baltic herring), you need a mild snaps.

The basic flavours of the smörgåsbord mainly comprise salinity, sweetness and acidity, and, in principle, no bitterness. This is why beer, with its gentle bitterness, makes such an ideal companion all the way through the smörgåsbord. If certain parts of the smörgåsbord are excluded, drinking wine all the way is equally feasible. Some say that white wines with high acidility, or indeed champagne, can even win the hearts of pickled herring, but I would still advise you to skip the wine, at least for the first – herring – round. Spicy white wines, in certain cases with a little residual sweetness, are preferable with salmon and fish. Soft, full-bodied reds, such as a pinot noir or a gently vinified shiraz, go well with meat. As I say, you can drink wine with certain parts of the smörgåsbord and get away with it, but as elevators of taste in this connection, beer and snaps take a lot of beating.

A word of advice. Use small snaps glasses, preferably no more than 2 cl, with four fillings. Most of the rounds include a variety of flavours, which in turn really call for different snaps varieties. With small glasses holding 1 or 2 cl, you can afford to drink the "right" snaps with each little item on your plate.

Round 1
Herring and Baltic herring
Generally speaking, herring is the loudest-flavoured part of the smörgåsbord. Pickled herring compositions in clear pickling medium are usually stronger than those in creamy sauce and require an assertive snaps. A milder snaps, such as Skåne, which has only half the spiciness of O. P. Anderson, goes well with the milder, creamy forms of pickled herring.

A snaps for strong herring: caraway-flavoured *brännvin*, such as O. P. Anderson or Aalborg Taffel.

A snaps for mild and creamy herring: a milder snaps, flavoured with caraway or dill, such as Skåne, Läckö Slottsaquavit or Aalborg Jubileum.

Round 2
Salmon and other fish
Fish recipes vary in spiciness and strength. Marinated fish can be of almost herring-like pungency, in which case your snaps must be chosen accordingly. Smoked fish can find an affinity to oaked snaps, with similar overtones of smoking and roasting, sherry and whisky tones from oaking and caraway. Dill-flavoured snaps always goes well with poached fish and shellfish.

A snaps for marinated fish: a flowery, aromatic snaps like Hallands Fläder or a robust, dill-flavoured one like, say, Aalborg Jubileum.

A snaps for smoked fish: caraway snaps varieties with a trace of oaking, such as Herrgårds Aquavit, Gammal Norrlands Akvavit, Aalborg Nordguld and Linie Aquavit.

A snaps for mild-flavoured fish and shellfish: dill-flavoured snaps, such as Läckö Slottsaquavit or Aalborg Jubileum.

Round 3
Cold cuts
Another congeries of flavours, including everything from the smoked, salted and slightly stronger meat and sausage recipes to the more mild-flavoured chicken and turkey. An oaked snaps with a roasted flavour will go excellently with the smoked items. Östgöta Sädes is made up of malt whisky which has been stored in bourbon casks and then mixed with pure spirit. In it we find a roundness of raisins and honey tones that harmonise with the meat.

A snaps for meat, sausage and smoked recipes: snaps with a touch of oaking, such as Östgöta Sädes Brännvin, Herrgårds Aquavit, Aalborg Nordguld and Linie Aquavit.
A snaps for chicken and turkey: mild snaps varieties like Skåne and Hallands Fläder.

Round 4
"Small warms"
Perhaps the Achilles heel of snaps – a round including both mild and strong flavours. Here we have the full gamut from the gentle mildness of *lutfisk* to the somewhat raunchier character of the meatballs and spare ribs.

A snaps for lutfisk: unflavoured snaps, such as Renat Brännvin or vodka.

A snaps for meatballs and chipolatas: aromatically flavoured snaps, such as Porsbrännvin (*pors* is bog myrtle).

A snaps for meat fried or roasted on the outside: one with stronger caraway flavouring and (recommended) a touch of oaking. O. P. Anderson, Herrgårds Akvavit,

Gammal Norrlands Akvavit and Aalborg Nordguld.

A snaps for Jansson's Temptation: one with softer caraway flavouring, such as Skåne, or an aromatic one like Hallands Fläder.

Round 5
The green round

Dill-flavoured snaps is an ideal companion for green vegetables: its rounded floridity and their softness of taste have all the makings of a happy marriage. For roasted or garlic-flavoured vegetables you need a caraway snaps.

A snaps for mild-flavoured vegetables: softer flavourings like those of dill-flavoured Läckö Slottsaquavit or Hallands Fläder.

A snaps for roasted vegetables: a stronger-flavoured caraway snaps like O. P. Anderson or Aalborg Taffel.

Round 6
Cheese

Caraway and cheese are a classic partnership. By the same token, all kinds of snaps go well with matured hard cheeses.

A snaps for matured hard cheese: all kinds of snaps, especially the caraway-flavoured ones.

A snaps for white mould cheese: snaps flavoured with Seville orange, such as Årsta Brännvin, Rånäs Brännvin.

Round 7
Dessert

As mentioned earlier, most kinds of snaps have no sweetness. But the sugar is already present in the dessert, and a fruit snaps turns almost into a liqueur when coupled with the sweetness of a dessert, and especially together with dark chocolate.

A snaps for dessert: snaps flavoured with fruit or soft fruit, such as Årsta Brännvin, Rånäs Brännvin, Svartvinbärsbrännvin (black currant) or, from Denmark, Emma Brøndums Skovbærbrændevin.

Round 8
Coffee, biscuits and confectionery

The fruit in the Seville snaps conveys a Calvados feeling, but coffee will also be excellently partnered by oaked snaps.

A snaps for coffee, biscuits and confectionery: Seville-flavoured, like Årsta and Rånäs Brännvin or oaked like Östgöta Sädes, Aalborg Nordguld, Herrgårds Aquavit, Norrlands Akvavit or Linie Aquavit.

Herring and Baltic herring

Herring (*sill*) is the mainstay of the smörgåsbord. With its sweet-and-sour savours and accompanied by Baltic herring (*strömming*) it inaugurates the first of eight rounds in your smörgåsbord odyssey. Here we present forty-odd recipes for herring and Baltic herring: clear, creamy, pickled and in casseroles.

From the salt water off the west coast to the brackish water off Kalmar it is called *sill* (herring), after which its name changes to *strömming* (Baltic herring). *Sill* is a tad fatter and longer than *strömming*, presumably due to the difference in the salinity of their habitats, but basically they are one and the same fish. Herring has been part of our staple diet ever since the heyday of herring fishing in 16th century Bohuslän, when it would appear off the coast in vast shoals.

Classic pickled herring

10–20 servings

5 herring fillets, pre-soaked
1 dl distilled vinegar (*ättika*,
12% strength)
2 dl caster sugar
3 dl water
½ red onion, sliced
½ onion, sliced
1 small carrot, sliced
8 allspice corns
1 bay leaf
Garnish:
red onion rings
crushed allspice corns

► Bring the *ättika*, sugar,
water, red onion, carrot, allspice and bay leaf to the boil
and stir till the sugar dissolves.
Leave to cool.
   Put the drained herring fillets in the pickling liquid and
store in the fridge for at least 2
days. Serve the herring cut up
in pieces and garnished with
red onion rings and crushed
allspice corns.

Emma's herring (Brantevik)

20 servings

1 kg fillets of Baltic herring
with the skin removed
Pickling medium:
6 dl water
1 dl distilled vinegar (*ättika*,
12% strength)
2 tbsp salt
2 onions
2 red onions
3 dl caster sugar
4 bay leaves
1 dl chopped dill
40 allspice corns
40 black peppercorns

40 white peppercorns
1 tsp lemon pepper
► Day 1: Bring the water, *ättika*
and salt to the boil. Leave to
cool. Put in the Baltic herring
and leave overnight.
   Day 2: Remove the Baltic
herring from the liquid and
wipe it dry in a tea towel.
Peel and chop the onion.
Crumble the bay leaves. Place
alternate layers of herring and
onion + spices in a jar or dish.
Refrigerate for 2 days while it
matures.

Herring & Baltic herring

Pickling herring

Put the herring to soak: Put the salted herring filets in a mixing bowl. Pour on enough cold water to reach 5-10 cm above the herring. Refrigerate overnight. The exact time depends on the size of the herring and the preferred salinity. Taste the herring at the thick end, to decide whether it is ready or needs more soaking. Never rinse the herring under the cold tap, because if you do it may very well tear or go soft on you.

You can also buy your herring pre-soaked, which saves time on the recipes given here. Sometimes, though, the pre-soaked variety can be over-salty, so put it to soak in water for an hour or else overnight.

Take care not to overdo the soaking, because then the herring will turn soft and ragged, apart from which, if you soak away too much of the salt you may be inviting a bacteria problem.

Cutting the herring

When cutting up herring, always trim away the belly part and the tail end, as well as any soft parts. This way your filet will be straight, handsome and firm-fleshed. Having trimmed your filet, you can choose between cutting it up into large or small pieces.

The pickling medium

"1–2–3" is a classic pickling medium, meaning one part distilled vinegar (*ättika* in Swedish, 12% strength), 2 parts caster sugar and 3 parts water. With this formula you can adjust the quantity of pickling medium to the amount of herring you are pickling.

The seasoning for this basic medium can vary, but the commonest ingredients are carrot, onion and bay leaf, though you can also add cloves, cinnamon,

ginger, black pepper, green cardamom, etc. Most often you make a basic pickling medium with simple seasoning and pickle a fairly large quantity of herring. After a day or two you can change the medium and use different flavourings of berries, herbs, spices or creamy sauces. It's a good idea to reserve a little of the pickling medium for serving, because then you can serve the herring in a beautifully clear liquid. Take care to follow the recipe for basic pickling medium closely, so that the herring will keep longer. Take care also to use only clean tools and vessels when working with herring. Pickled herring, properly handled, will keep for up to a fortnight in the fridge.

Filleting Baltic herring

To fillet Baltic herring, start at the join in the centre, nearest the head, of the spatchcocked "herring flounder" (as the Swedish term goes). Poke a fingernail in between the skin and flesh to part them, and then pull the flesh away from the skin down towards the tail.

Herring pickling medium, basic recipe

Enough for 1 kg soaked herring filets
10–20 servings
2 dl distilled vinegar (*ättika*, 12% strength)
4 dl caster sugar
6 dl water
1 bay leaf
14–16 allspice corns
6 cloves
2 small carrots, sliced
1 yellow or red onion, sliced
► Mix the *ättika*, water and sugar together and bring to the boil. Add the spices, carrots and onion. Leave to cool.

Cover the filets with the pickling medium and store in the fridge for at least 2 days. When draining the herring after-

wards, take care to use clean utensils. Dry the herring with kitchen tissue and cut it into serving portions. The herring must be dry when you put it into the creamy sauces, because otherwise the sauce may get too thin or the pickling medium may turn cloudy.

Basic pickling medium recipe for Baltic herring

Make sure the herring is white all through after immersion in the pickling medium, because otherwise it's still raw in the middle, which can affect its storage life.

Enough for 1 kg Baltic herring filets
10–20 servings
7½ dl water
1½ dl distilled vinegar (*ättika*, 12% strength)
1 tbsp salt
► Mix the pickling medium ingredients together and bring to the boil. Leave to cool.

Immerse the filets in the pickling medium and refrigerate overnight, until the herring is white and firm. Pour off the pickling medium and put the herring to drain well in a colander.

Use clean utensils and vessels. If the filets are too big you can split them down the middle

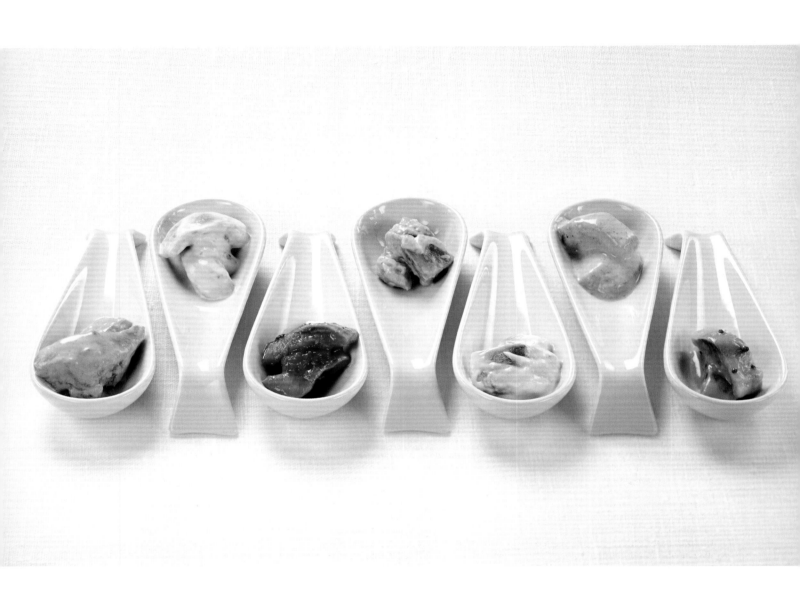

Roasted paprika herring

10–20 servings

4–5 pickled herring filets, cut up in pieces
1 dl soured cream (*gräddfil*)
1 dl yoghurt naturel, 10 %
2 tbsp mayonnaise
½ tbsp chilli sauce
1 tsp Dijon mustard
2 tsp smoked paprika powder
1 tsp pressed lemon
salt

► Mix the *gräddfil*, mayonnaise, chilli sauce and Dijon mustard into a creamy sauce. Stir in the paprika powder. Add lemon juice and salt to taste. Remember the herring is already salted. Fold the herring into the sauce. Transfer to a clean glass jar and refrigerate for about 12 hours, to bring out the flavours.

Lime and coriander herring

10–20 servings

4–5 pickled herring filets, cut up in pieces
1 dl crème fraîche
1 dl mayonnaise
1 dl yoghurt naturel, 10 %
1 tbsp sweet chilli sauce
½ lime, juice and grated zest of
1 clove of garlic, grated
1 tbsp chopped coriander
salt (optional)

► Mix the crème fraîche, mayonnaise and yoghurt together. Beat in the chilli sauce, lime juice and zest and garlic. Add the coriander and mix with a stick blender. Add salt to taste, bearing in mind that the herring is already salted. Fold the herring into the sauce. Transfer to a clean glass jar and refrigerate for about 12 hours, to bring out the flavours.

Smoked tomato herring

10–20 servings

4–5 pickled herring filets, cut up in pieces
1 dl rapeseed oil
3 thyme stalks
50 g smoked side pork, diced
2 cloves of garlic, chopped
1½ dl strained tomatoes
½ dl sun-dried tomatoes
1 tbsp honey
1 tbsp red wine vinegar
½ lemon, grated zest of
salt
black pepper

► Pour the oil into a saucepan and add the thyme, side pork and garlic. Simmer gently for about 30 minutes. Remove from the heat and put to one side for the oil to cool, with the pork and spices still in it. Strain the oil at room temperature.

Mix the strained tomatoes, sun-dried tomatoes, honey and red wine vinegar together in a food processor. Add the oil in a thin jet with the machine still running. Add grated lemon zest, salt and black pepper to taste. Fold the herring into the sauce. Transfer to a clean glass jar and refrigerate for about 12 hours, to bring out the flavours.

Madras curry herring

10–20 servings

4–5 pickled herring filets, cut up in pieces
1 apple
1 shallot
1 tbsp butter
1 tbsp Madras curry
1 dl crème fraîche
1 tbsp mayonnaise
1 tbsp mango chutney
salt
black pepper
a little pressed lemon juice (optional)

► Peel and de-core the apple

and cut it in pieces. Peel and chop the shallot. Melt the butter in a pan over a medium flame. Sauté the apple and onion in butter together with the curry until they soften. Leave to cool. Run the apple mixture in the food processor together with the crème fraîche, mayonnaise and mango chutney. Add salt and black pepper to taste, and perhaps too a little pressed lemon juice. Fold the herring into the sauce. Transfer to a clean glass jar and refrigerate for about 12 hours, to bring out the flavours.

Lemon herring

10–20 servings

4–5 pickled herring filets, cut up in pieces
1 dl crème fraîche
1 dl mayonnaise
1 dl soured cream (*gräddfil*)
1 tbsp Dijon mustard
2 lemons, grated zest of
1 lemon, pressed juice of
salt
Tabasco (optional)

► Mix the crème fraîche, mayonnaise, *gräddfil* and Dijon mustard together into a smooth sauce. Add the grated lemon zest and the lemon juice. Season with salt and (optional) Tabasco. Fold the herring into the sauce. Transfer to a clean glass jar and refrigerate for about 12 hours, to bring out the flavours.

Tandoori herring

10–20 servings

4–5 pickled herring filets, cut up in pieces
2 dl yoghurt naturel, 10 %
1 dl mayonnaise
2 tbsp tandoori spice
2 tbsp honey
1 tsp pressed lemon juice
salt

► Mix the yoghurt, mayonnaise, tandoori spice and honey together. Add pressed lemon juice and salt to taste.

Fold the herring into the sauce. Transfer to a clean glass jar and refrigerate for about 12 hours, to bring out the flavours.

Mustard sauce (basic recipe)

10–20 servings

1 dl Swedish mustard
1 dl caster sugar
4 tbsp white wine vinegar
1 tbsp honey
2 dl rapeseed oil
1 tsp salt
about 1 tsp Demerara sugar
1 tbsp cold filter coffee

► Mix the mustard, sugar, vinegar and honey together. Beat until the sugar dissolves and the sauce is smooth. Add the oil, first a drop at a time and then in a fine jet while whisking. Add salt, Demerara sugar and coffee to taste. Worth knowing: The mustard sauce left over can be made into head waiter's sauce to go with the salmon; simply add chopped dill according to taste.

Mustard herring

10–20 servings

4–5 pickled herring filets, cut up in pieces
½ tsp brown mustard seeds
3 dl mustard sauce

► Put the mustard seeds in boiling water. Drain and leave to cool. Mix the mustard sauce with the mustard seeds. Fold the herring into the sauce. Transfer to a clean glass jar and refrigerate for about 12 hours, to bring out the flavours.

Photo from left to right: roasted paprika herring, lime and coriander herring, smoked tomato herring, madras curry herring, lemon herring, tandoori herring, mustard herring.

Rose-hip and green cardamom herring

10–20 servings

4–5 pickled herring filets, cut up in pieces
1 carrot
½ white onion
2 tbsp dried rose-hip husks
1 bay leaf
6 crushed green cardamom capsules
6 white peppercorns
2 cm ginger, thinly sliced
about 5 dl pickling medium, strained

► Peel and dice the carrot. Peel the white onion and cut it in strips. Put alternate layers of herring, rose hips, spices and vegetables into a clean glass jar. Pour on the pickling medium and refrigerate for about 12 hours, to bring out the flavours.

Pickled herring with star anise

10–20 servings

4–5 pickled herring filets, cut up in pieces
1 carrot
1 white onion
1 bay leaf
2 star anises
6 white peppercorns
about 5 dl pickling medium, strained

► Peel the carrot and cut it in strips. Peel the white onion and cut it into thin wedges. Put alternate layers of herring, vegetables and spices into a clean glass jar. Pour on the pickling medium and refrigerate for about 12 hours, to bring out the flavours.

Vanilla and lime-leaf herring

10–20 servings

4–5 pickled herring filets, cut up in pieces
½ yellow carrot
1 shallot
1 vanilla pod
about 5 dl pickling medium, strained
3 lime leaves
1 bay leaf
6 white peppercorns

► Peel the carrot and cut into small cubes. Peel and slice the shallot. Split the vanilla pod and scrape out the seeds. Stir the seeds into the pickling medium. Put alternate layers of herring, vegetables, vanilla pod, lime leaves, bay leaf and white pepper into a clean glass jar. Pour on the pickling medium and refrigerate for about 12 hours, to bring out the flavours.

Rowanberry herring

10–20 servings

4–5 pickled herring filets, cut up in pieces
½ yellow carrot
1 small onion
½ vanilla pod
about 5 dl pickling medium, strained
1 dl deep-frozen rowanberries
1 bay leaf
6 white peppercorns
1 tsp grated fresh ginger
½ tsp coriander seeds
½ tsp fennel seeds

► Peel the carrot and cut it into small cubes. Peel and slice the onion. Split the vanilla pod and scrape out the seeds. Stir the seeds into the pickling medium. Put alternate layers of herring, vegetables, vanilla pod, rowanberries and spices into a thoroughly cleaned glass jar. Pour on the pickling medium and refrigerate for about 12 hours, to bring out the flavours.

Sea buckthorn herring

10–20 servings

4–5 pickled herring filets, cut up in pieces
½ carrot
½ shallot
1 lemon grass stalk
1 dl sea buckthorn
6 black peppercorns
1 bay leaf
about 5 dl pickling medium, strained

► Peel and dice the carrot. Peel and slice the shallot. Slice the lower part of the lemon grass. Put alternate layers of herring, vegetables, lemon grass, sea buckthorn and spices into a clean glass jar. Pour on the pickling medium and refrigerate for about 12 hours, to bring out the flavours.

Lingonberry and black pepper herring

10–20 servings

4–5 pickled herring filets, cut up in pieces
½ carrot
½ white onion
1 tbsp honey
about 5 dl pickling medium, strained
1 dl deep-frozen lingonberries
12–15 black peppercorns
1 bay leaf

► Peel and dice the carrot. Peel the white onion and cut it into thing wedges. Stir the honey into the pickling medium. Put alternate layers of herring, vegetables, lingonberries and spices into a clean glass jar. Pour on the pickling medium and refrigerate for about 12 hours, to bring out the flavours.

Clear sherry herring

10–20 servings

4–5 matjes herring filets, cut up in pieces
½ dl distilled vinegar (*ättika*, 12% strength)
1 dl caster sugar
¾ dl water
¾ dl dry sherry
½ yellow carrot
1 shallot
2 bay leaves
6–8 white peppercorns

► Bring the *ättika*, sugar, water and sherry to the boil and stir until the sugar has dissolved. Leave to cool. Peel and dice the carrot. Peel and chop the shallot. Put alternate layers of matjes herring, vegetables and spices into a clean glass jar. Pour on the pickling medium and refrigerate for about 12 hours, to bring out the flavours.

Photo from left to right: rose-hip and green cardamom herring, pickled herring with star anise, vanilla and lime leaf herring, rowanberry herring, sea buckthorn herring, lingonberry and black pepper herring, clear sherry herring.

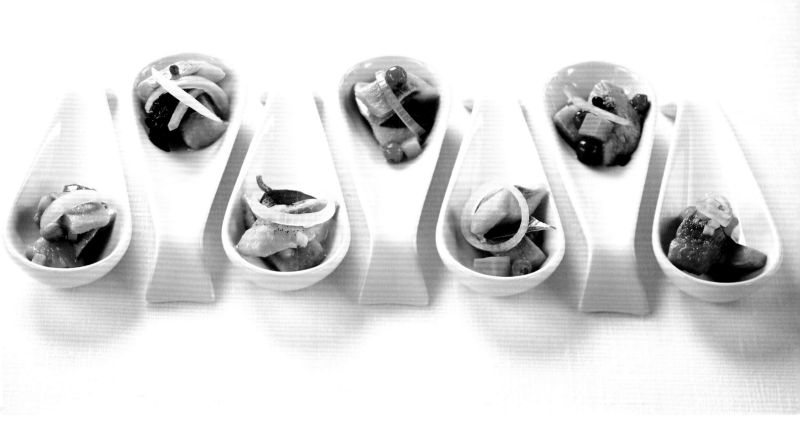

Crown dill herring

10–20 servings

4–5 pickled herring filets, cut up in pieces
1 small carrot
1 shallot
4 dill crowns
1 tsp dill seeds
1 bay leaf
6 white peppercorns
about 5 dl pickling medium, strained

► Peel the carrot and cut it into small cubes. Peel and slice the shallot. Put alternate layers of herring, carrot, onion, crown dill, dill seeds, bay leaf and white peppercorns in the pickling medium into a clean glass jar. Pour on the pickling medium and refrigerate for about 12 hours, to bring out the flavours.

Herring pickled in coarse mustard and capers

10–20 servings

4–5 pickled herring filets, cut up in pieces
1 shallot
1 bay leaf
3 tbsp capers
1 dl cider vinegar mustard or some other coarse, acidulous mustard
about 5 dl pickling medium,

strained.
► Peel the shallot and chop small. Mix it with the bay leaf, capers and mustard. Stir into the pickling medium. Mix the herring and mustard pickling medium together. Transfer the herring to a clean glass jar. Pour on the pickling medium and refrigerate for about 12 hours, to bring out the flavours.

Black currant herring

10–20 servings
4–5 pickled herring filets, cut up in pieces
½ carrot
½ red onion
2 tbsp concentrated black currant juice
about 5 dl pickling medium, strained
1 dl black currants
1 bay leaf

► Peel the carrot and cut it into small cubes. Peel the red onion and cut it into thin wedges.

Mix the black currant juice with the pickling medium. Put alternate layers of herring, vegetables, black currants and bay leaf into a clean glass jar. Pour on the black currant pickling medium and refrigerate for about 12 hours, to bring out the flavours.

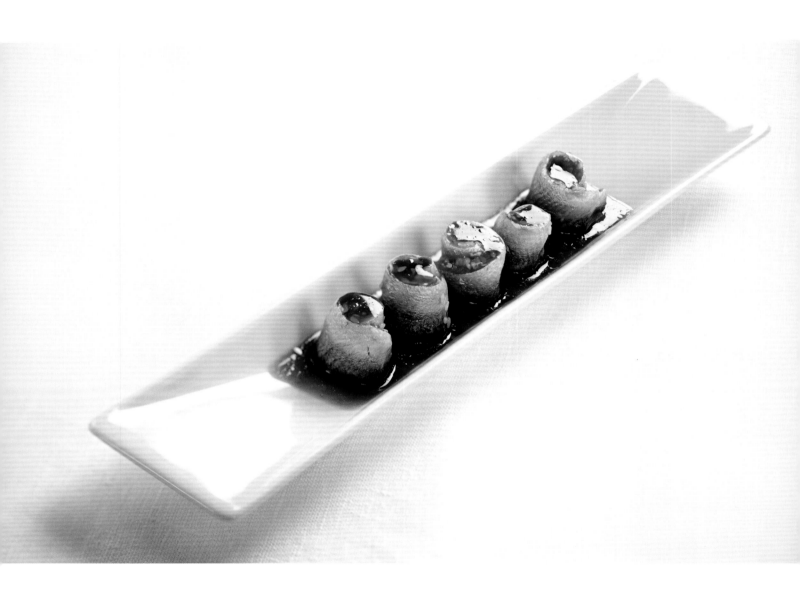

Teriyaki Baltic herring
10–20 servings
500 g Baltic herring, gutted and cleaned
1 tbsp olive oil
about 1 tsp salt
½ tbsp sesame oil
3 dl teriyaki sauce
1 tbsp black or white sesame seeds

► Set the oven to 175 ˚C. Cut away the dorsal fin and cut the herring lengthwise to make two filets. Roll it up, skin outermost, and place in an oiled oven-proof dish. Add salt. Mix the sesame oil and teriyaki sauce together and pour over the herring. Sprinkle with sesame seeds.

Bake in the middle of the oven for about 20 minutes. Remove and leave to cool in the sauce.

Matjes herring
10–20 servings
4–5 matjes herring filets
2 spring onions or ½ baby
leek
plucked dill
chopped chives
2 tbsp cold pressed rape-
seed oil
black pepper, milled

► Dry the matjes herring filets in kitchen tissue and cut them into serving portions. Shred the spring onion. Distribute this, the chives and the dill over the matjes filets. Drizzle with rapeseed oil, followed by one or two twists of the peppermill.

Fried pickled Baltic herring

10–20 servings

500 g Baltic herring, gutted and cleaned
1½ dl fine-ground rye flour
1 tsp salt
1 pinch of milled white pepper
about 50 g salted butter for frying
2 shallots
1 carrot
about 1 litre pickling medium, strained
1 bay leaf
12–15 cloves
8 allspice corns

▶ Cut the dorsal fin off the herring. Rinse the herring and drain well. Mix the rye flour, salt and pepper together on a plate. Fold the herring and dredge it in the mixture. Fry the filets for about 3 minutes in butter until they are golden brown. Leave to cool. Peel and slice the shallot and carrot. Bring the pickling medium and spices to the boil. Leave to cool. Put alternate layers of herring and vegetables into clean glass jars. Pour on the pickling medium and refrigerate for about 12 hours, to bring out the flavours.

Baltic herring pickled in bleak roe

10–20 servings

500 g pickled filets of Baltic herring
1 dl mayonnaise
1 dl crème fraîche
1 dl soured cream (*gräddfil*)
1 tbsp Dijon mustard
1 tbsp white wine vinegar
3–5 dashes of Tabasco
salt
4 tbsp bleak roe, preferably from Kalix

▶ Dry the Baltic herring in kitchen tissue. Stir the mayonnaise, crème fraîche, *gräddfil* and Dijon mustard into a smooth sauce. Add the white wine vinegar and Tabasco. Add salt to taste. Fold the Baltic herring into the sauce. Transfer to clean glass jars and refrigerate for about 12 hours, to bring out the flavours. Carefully fold the bleak roe into the Baltic herring before serving.

Mustard and gherkin Baltic herring

10–20 servings

500 g pickled filets of Baltic herring
2 boiled eggs
1 tbsp sherry vinegar
2 tbsp Dijon mustard
1 dl olive oil
1 shallot, chopped fine
½ dl gherkins, chopped
2 tbsp capers
salt
pepper
2 tbsp chopped parsley

▶ Shell the eggs. Mix the eggs, vinegar and Dijon mustard with a stick blender. Add the oil a drop at a time and run to a smooth sauce (the stick blender again). Add the shallot, gherkins and capers. Add salt and pepper to taste. Fold in the Baltic herring. Transfer to clean glass jars and refrigerate for about 12 hours, to bring out the flavours. Carefully fold the parsley into the Baltic herring before serving.

Baltic herring pickled in herbs

10–20 servings

500 g pickled filets of Baltic herring
1 dl mayonnaise
1 dl crème fraîche
1 dl soured cream (*gräddfil*)
1 tbsp white wine vinegar
1 tbsp Dijon mustard
4 tbsp fresh herbs, e.g. dill, flat-leafed parsley, basil and rocket
25 g fresh spinach
2 cloves of garlic
3–5 dashes of Tabasco
salt

▶ Mix the mayonnaise, crème fraîche, *gräddfil*, vinegar and Dijon mustard into a smooth sauce. Take a little of the sauce and mix it with the herbs and spinach, using a stick blender. Return this to the main body of the sauce. Peel the garlic, grate it on the fine side of the grater and fold into the sauce. Add Tabasco and salt to taste. Carefully fold in the Baltic herring filets. Transfer to clean glass jars and refrigerate for about 12 hours, to bring out the flavours.

Baltic herring pickled in citrus fruits

10–20 servings

500 g filets of Baltic herring
1 tbsp sea salt
4 lemons, pressed juice of
½ lemon, grated zest of
½ orange, grated zest of
½ lime, grated zest of
2 bay leaves, crushed
3 dl good-quality olive oil

▶ Put the filets of Baltic herring into a dish. Sprinkle with sea salt and pour on the lemon juice. Refrigerate for about 6 hours. The herring flesh must be white all the way through. Remove the herring and wipe it with kitchen tissue. Put layers of herring, grated lemon zest and bay leaf into a clean glass jar and cover with olive oil. Refrigerate for about 12 hours, to bring out the flavours.

Leave the Baltic herring at room temperature for about 2 hours before serving, to give the oil time to melt.

Photo from top left: fried pickled Baltic herring, mustard and gherkin Baltic herring, Baltic herring pickled in bleak roe, Baltic herring pickled in herbs, Baltic herring pickled in citrus fruits.

Baltic herring with bread and pine nuts

10–20 servings

500 g Baltic herring, gutted and cleaned
3 tbsp pine nuts
1½ dl dried bread crumbs
2 dl olive oil
3 tbsp yellow raisins, chopped
2 tbsp chopped parsley
1 orange, grated zest of
1 lemon, grated zest of
1 tsp salt
1 pinch of black pepper

► Set the oven to 175 ˚C. Cut away the dorsal fin and cut the herring lengthwise to make two filets. Place the herring skin side downwards on the worktop.

Roast the pine nuts in a dry frying pan until they are golden brown. Add the dried bread crumbs and roast for 5-10 seconds. Drizzle with half the olive oil and sauté the breadcrumbs until they stick together. Remove the pan from the heat and mix in the raisins, parsley and grated orange and lemon zest. Season the herring with salt and pepper.

Put a small spoonful of breadcrumb mixture onto each filet. Roll the fillets up and place them in an oiled oven-proof dish. Sprinkle the remaining breadcrumb mixture over the filets and drizzle them with the rest of the olive oil. Bake in the middle of the oven for about 20 minutes. Remove and leave to cool.

BBQ Baltic herring

10–20 servings

500 g Baltic herring, gutted and cleaned
Spicy sauce:
2½ tbsp Worcester sauce
2½ tbsp Japanese soy
1 tsp allspice
1 tsp chilli pepper
1 tsp basil
1 tsp oregano
1 tsp black pepper
1 tsp fresh grated ginger
1 tsp mustard powder
½ dl apple cider vinegar
BBQ sauce:
2½ dl crushed tomatoes
3 tbsp butter
¾ dl pressed lemon
1 dl peaches, chopped in the food processor
1–2 drops liquid smoke
½ dl Demerara sugar
½ dl chilli sauce, ketchup type
1 tbsp bourbon
about 1 tsp salt
1 pinch black pepper

► Mix all the ingredients for the spicy sauce, then mix this with the ingredients for the barbeque sauce. Cover and cook gently for about 2 hours. Season with salt and pepper. Leave the sauce to cool and refrigerate it overnight.

Set the oven to 175 ˚C. Cut away the dorsal fin and cut the herring lengthwise to make two filets. Roll them up, skin side inwards. Place the herring in an oven-proof dish and cover with the barbeque sauce. Bake in the middle of the oven for about 20 minutes. Remove and leave to cool.

Herring pickled in Mackmyra whisky

10–20 servings
4–5 matjes herring filets, cut up in pieces
½ dl distilled vinegar (*ättika*, 12% strength)
1 dl caster sugar
¾ dl water
¾ dl Mackmyra whisky
1 shallot
1 bay leaf
4 white peppercorns
1 tbsp chopped dill
► Bring the *ättika*, sugar, water and whisky to the boil and stir till the sugar is dissolved. Leave to cool.

Peel and shred the shallot. Dry the matjes herring with kitchen tissue and put it into a clean glass jar together with the onion, spices and whisky mixture. Refrigerate for about 12 hours, to bring out the flavours. Fold chopped dill into the herring before serving.

Housewife's herring

10–20 servings
4–5 matjes herring filets, cut up in pieces
3 dl soured cream (*gräddfil*)
2 tbsp mayonnaise
½ tbsp chilli sauce
1 tsp Dijon mustard
2 dashes of Tabasco
salt
2 small boiled eggs
1 spring onions
Garnish:
1 boiled egg
shredded spring onion
► Cut up the matjes herring in pieces and dry it on kitchen tissue. Mix the *gräddfil*, mayonnaise, chilli sauce and Dijon mustard into a creamy sauce. Add Tabasco and salt to taste, bearing in mind that the herring is already salted. Shell the eggs and chop them small. Shred the spring onion. Fold the herring, egg and spring onion into the sauce. Transfer the herring to a clean glass jar. Pour on the pickling medium and refrigerate for about 12 hours, to bring out the flavours. Garnish with chopped boiled eggs and shredded spring onion.

Baltic herring with saffron and other spices

500 g Baltic herring, cleaned and filleted
2 tsp rapeseed oil
1 tsp salt
1 shallot
1 carrot
½ tsp fennel seeds
½ tsp coriander seeds
1 stick of cinnamon
1 pinch of saffron
1 tsp cider vinegar
1 tsp white balsamic vinegar
1 dl olive oil
sea salt

► Set the oven to 150° C. Cut off the dorsal fin and divide the herring lengthwise to make two filets. Roll the filets up, skin side outwards. Brush an oven-proof dish with oil. Put the rolled-up Baltic herring filets into it, not too close together. Salt them and bake them on the middle shelf of the oven for 12–15 minutes. Peel the shallot and carrot and slice them thin before mixing with the spices, vinegar and oil in a saucepan. Heat gently for about 5 minutes, until the shallot and carrot have softened. The spices will then discharge their flavours into the marinade. Spoon the marinade over the fish.

Serve immediately or store in the fridge. The fish will keep in the fridge for 2 days if covered by the marinade.

Caviar Baltic herring

10–20 servings
500 g Baltic herring, gutted and cleaned
1 tbsp butter
1 onion, chopped small
½–1 tsp salt
Sauce:
2 tbsp lightly smoked caviar
2 dl whipping cream
3 egg yolks
2 tbsp chopped dill
► Set the oven to 175 ˚C. Cut away the dorsal fin and cut the herring lengthwise to make two filets. Rinse and drain. Grease an oven-proof dish with butter and sprinkle the bottom with onion chopped small. Roll the filets up, skin side outwards, and place them in the dish. Salt them.

Mix the caviar, cream, egg yolks and dill together. Pour the sauce over the herring. Bake in the middle of the oven for about 20 minutes.

Spiced Swedish anchovy

10–12 servings

2 tins of Swedish anchovy filets, 125 g each
2 red onions
4 tbsp chives, shredded
Marinade:
½ dl rapeseed oil
4 drops of Tabasco
1 clove of garlic, grated small
2 tbsp Japanese soy
5 cm fresh ginger, grated small
1 tbsp liquid honey
2 tbsp pressed lemon

▶ Mix the marinade ingredients together and pour over the Swedish anchovy.

Marinate for about 4 hours in the fridge. Remove the anchovies from the marinade. Strain the marinade. Arrange the anchovies on a serving dish. Peel the onion and chop small. Sprinkle red onion and chives over the anchovies and pour on the marinade.

Matjes herring tartar

10–20 servings

2 fillets of matjes herring
½ apple
½ red onion
4 radishes
½ salted cucumber
1 tbsp chives, chopped
3 tbsp crème fraîche
Garnish:
sprigs of dill

► Cut up the herring. Peel, de-core and dice the apple. Peel the onion and chop small. Top and tail the radishes and dice them. Chop the salted cucumber. Mix the herring, apple, radishes, onion, cucumber, chives and crème fraîche together. Make eggs with the tartar and garnish with sprigs of dill.

Egg halves with bleak roe
20 servings
10 small eggs
100 g bleak roe
1 tbsp shred lemonzest
► Put the eggs into boiling
water and boil them for 10 minutes. Chill them in iced water.
Shell them and halve them
crosswise, cutting off the ends
so that the halves will stand
firmly.

Garnish each half-egg with a
dash of bleak roe and lemonzest.

Egg halves with shrimp mixture

20 servings
10 small eggs
100 g peeled shrimps
½ dl mayonnaise
1 tsp white wine vinegar
1 tsp Dijon mustard
1 tsp grated horseradish
4 sprigs of dill, chopped
salt
20 shrimps for garnish

► Put the eggs into boiling water and boil them for 10 minutes. Chill them in iced water. Shell them and halve them crosswise, cutting off the ends so that the halves will stand firmly.

Wipe the shrimps dry with kitchen tissue. Reserve a few for garnish and rough-chop the rest. Stir the mayonnaise, white wine vinegar, Dijon mustard and horseradish together. Mix the sauce, a little at a time, with the shrimps to the right consistency. The shrimp mixture must be firm but not wet. Stir in the chopped dill. Add salt to taste. Garnish the egg-halves with the shrimp mixture and one shrimp each.

Salmon and other fish

Our Swedish salmon is of high quality. Tore Wretman described it as unusually fat and tender but still firm-fleshed, and he would only use Swedish salmon on his guest performances the world over. It is hard to believe that once upon a time being spared salmon at least once or twice a week was a perk for servant maids and farmhands. The emphasis of the second round is on salmon – poached, smoked and salted – but the el too has its appointed place on the smörgåsbord. The saying goes that a genuine eel feast (*ålagille*) is only to be had in an eel fisher's boathouse by the sea between Åhus and Yngsjö. Any other arrangement is merely a party with eel thrown in.

Gravlax cured in aniseed and Norrlands snaps

10–20 servings

1 kg fresh salmon – the middle part, skin removed
¾ dl caster sugar
½ dl salt
1 tsp coarse-milled white peppercorns
1 tbsp aniseed
1 tbsp fennel seeds
1 tbsp caraway
4 cl Norrlands Akvavit (snaps)

► Day 1: Trim the salmon smooth, removing all bones and membranes. Cut it lengthwise into two oblong pieces. Mix the sugar, salt and pepper for pickling. Rub this mixture into the pieces of salmon. Crush the aniseed, fennel seeds and caraway gently in a mortar and sprinkle them over the salmon. Drizzle with snaps. Put the filet of salmon into double plastic bags.

Leave for 1 hour at room temperature, to start the curing process. Store the salmon in the fridge between two plates, to put it under pressure. Leave to cure until next day.

Day 2: Remove the salmon and wipe it nearly dry with kitchen tissue, making sure the spices do not drop off. Put it in a new plastic bag and leave it to cure in the fridge for another day or two.

► *Salmon for gravlax should be stored in the freezer for at least two days, to kill off any parasites. Alternatively, prepare your gravlax immediately, leaving it in the pickling mixture for two days, and then give it at least two days in the freezer.*

Gravlax flavoured with orange and Szechuan pepper

10–20 servings

1 kg fresh salmon – the middle part, skin removed
¾ dl caster sugar
½ dl salt
1 tsp coarse-milled white peppercorns
1 orange, grated zest of
14–16 crushed Szechuan peppercorns
2 tbsp Grand Marnier

► Day 1: Trim and clean the salmon, removing all bones and membranes. Cut it lengthwise into two oblong pieces. Mix the sugar, salt and pepper for pickling. Rub this mixture into the pieces of salmon. Sprinkle with orange zest and Szechuan pepper. Drizzle with Grand Marnier. Put the filet of salmon into double plastic bags.

Leave for 1 hour at room temperature, to start the curing process. Store the salmon in the fridge between two plates, to put it under pressure. Leave to cure until next day.

Day 2: Remove the salmon and wipe it nearly dry with kitchen tissue, making sure the spices do not drop off. Put it in a new plastic bag and leave it to cure in the fridge for another day or two.

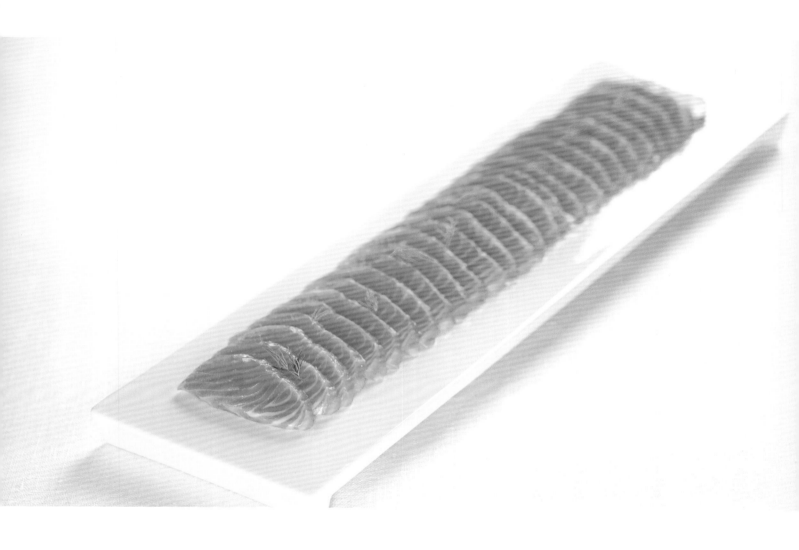

Gravlax cured in lemon and dill

10–20 servings

1 kg fresh salmon – the middle part, skin removed
¾ dl caster sugar
½ dl salt
1 tsp coarse-milled white peppercorns
1 lemon, grated zest of
12 crushed dill stalks

► Day 1: Trim the salmon smooth, removing all bones and membranes. Cut it lengthwise into two oblong pieces. Mix the sugar, salt and pepper for pickling. Rub this mixture into the pieces of salmon. Sprinkle with lemon zest and the dill stalks. Put the filet of salmon into double plastic bags. Leave for 1 hour at room temperature, to start the curing process. Store the salmon in the fridge between two plates, to put it under pressure. Leave to cure until next day.

Day 2: Remove the salmon and wipe it nearly dry with kitchen tissue, making sure the spices do not drop off. Put it in a new plastic bag and leave it to cure in the fridge for another day or two.

Lumpfish caviar and egg cream

10–20 servings
300 g lumpfish roe
1½ litres 7.5 % brine (75 g salt per 9¼ dl water)
Egg cream:
4 eggs
½ dl Dijon mustard
2 dl milk
40 g butter, cubed
salt

Garnish:
1 tbsp chives, chopped small
► Carefully squeeze and scrape the roe out of the sac. Try to remove as much of the sinews and membranes as possible without harming the eggs.

Divide up the brine, using 6-7 dl at a time. Put the roe into the brine and stir carefully with a whisk to remove the membranes from all the eggs. Repeat this until all the mem-branes have been removed. While you are stirring the roe in the brine, it will be pickled into the bargain. Keep stirring for about an hour. Season to taste, checking the salinity. If the roe tastes raw, leave it to pickle in the brine for a while longer before draining off the brine.

Use the caviar immediately or deep-freeze it in tight-fitting packages. It will keep for about 3 months in the freezer. Mix the eggs, mustard, milk and butter together in a saucepan, whisking over a low flame till you have a smooth cream. Remove from the heat and add salt to taste. Serve the egg cream in the egg shells, topped with caviar and chives.

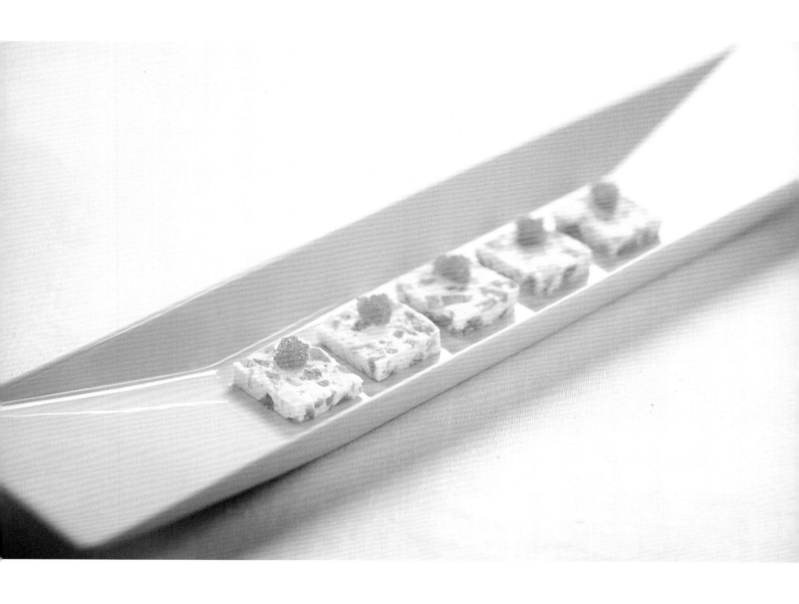

Salmon and green cheese terrine

10–20 servings

200 g cold-smoked salmon
200 g gravlax
4 sheets of gelatine
2 dl crème fraîche
1 dl Philadelphia cheese
Garnish: Kalix bleak roe

► Cut the salmon into cubes. Soak the sheets of gelatine in plenty of cold water for about 5 minutes. Mix the crème fraîche and Philadelphia cheese. Remove the gelatine from the water and melt it in 2 tbsp of the crème fraîche and cheese mixture over a low flame. Stir in the gelatine mixture together with the cubes of salmon. Pour this into a terrine mould lined with plastic foil and smooth the surface. Fold plastic foil over the mould and put a weight on top to keep the surface level. Refrigerate overnight. Before serving, the easiest way is to put it in the freezer for about 30 minutes and then tip it out and slice it through the plastic with a sharp knife.

Salmon tartar with quail's eggs

10 servings
300 g fresh salmon, belly part if possible, with skin and bones removed
1 small red onion
2 tbsp capers
5 quail's eggs
1 tbsp chives, chopped
1½ tbsp Dijon mustard
sea salt
black pepper

► Chop the salmon small. Peel the onion and chop it small. Chop the capers. Put the quail's eggs into boiling water and boil them for 3 minutes, plunging them straight into iced water afterwards. Mix the salmon with the red onion, capers, chives and mustard. Add salt and pepper to taste.

Shape the salmon into small pucks. Shell the eggs and halve them. Garnish with the egg halves. Give each tartar a slight twist of the peppermill.

Pie crust

30–40 small pie casings
500 g white flour
125 g butter
2 egg yolks
1¼ dl water
2 tsp salt
1 tsp caster sugar
For brushing:
whites of 2 eggs

► Mix all the ingredients for the dough in a dough mixer or food processor and run quickly into a dough. Cover this over with plastic foil and refrigerate overnight.

Set the oven to 175 °C. Roll the dough thin with a rolling pin or pasta machine. Press it into ramekins about 4 x 4 cm in diameter, with a small amount of dough hanging over the edges. Put an oven dish on top with a weight in it. Bake the casings in the middle of the oven and under pressure for about 2½ minutes. Remove them and trim the edges. Return to the oven and continue baking for 8 or 10 minutes, until they have turned a nice colour.

Lower the oven temperature to 90 °C. Allow the pie crusts to cool, then brush them with the beaten egg whites and bake for 3-4 minutes.

Worth knowing: The pastry, well wrapped up in plastic, can be stored in the freezer.

Rich short pastry with almonds

25–30 small pastry cases
4 tbsp + 1¼ dl white flour
60 g unsalted butter, at room temperature
¾ dl icing sugar
1 g salt (½ pinch)
1½ tbsp almond flour
½ medium-sized egg

► Sift 4 tbsp of the white flour. Mix the butter, sugar, salt, almond flour, egg and sifted white flour together into a dough. Sieve the remaining flour (1¼ dl) and fold it carefully into the dough. Put the dough into plastic foil and store in the fridge for at least an hour. Set the oven to 200 °C. Roll the pastry thin and use it to line pie moulds measuring 4 x 4 cm. Nick the pastry with a fork. Place an empty pie mould in the lined one and press down. Put weights in the pie moulds and store them in the freezer for about 20 minutes. Bake the pie casings, straight out of the freeze, in the middle of the oven for about 5 to 8 minutes, depending on whether they are to be completely or just half baked.

**Västerbotten cheese pie
with Kalix bleak roe**

12 servings

12 small pie casings, (see recipe p 51)
100 g Västerbotten cheese
1 dl crème fraîche
½ pinch or so of Cayenne pepper
1 tsp snaps (brännvin), e.g. Skåne

Garnish:
200 g bleak roe
10 leaves of sorrel
sea salt

► Grate the Västerbotten cheese and put it into a saucepan together with the crème fraîche. Melt over a low flame, stirring all the time so it doesn't burn. Season with Cayenne pepper, snaps and salt.

Pour the mixture into the pie casing and put it in the fridge for about 1 hour to set. Garnish the pie with bleak roe, sorrel and a little sea salt when serving.

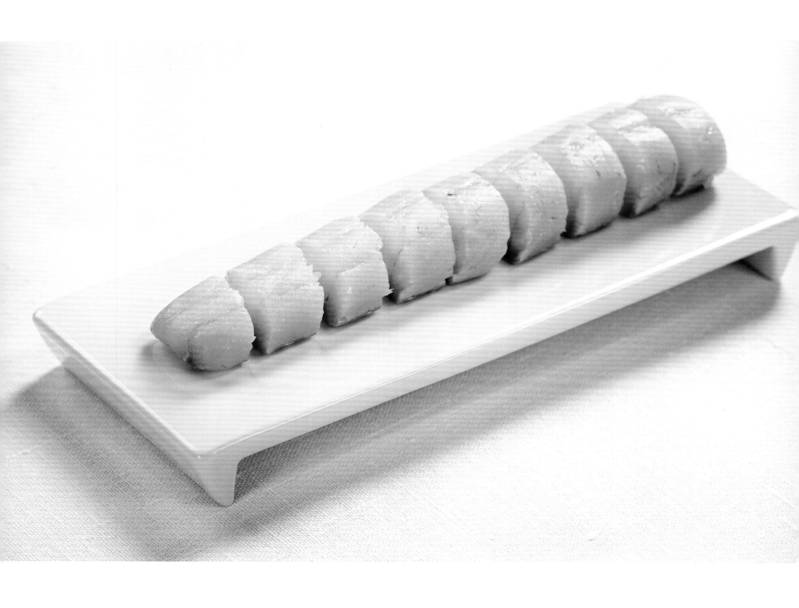

Smoked pike-perch

10–12 servings
500 g filet of pike-perch
9 ½ dl water
50 g salt
3 dl alder chips

► Remove all skin and bones from the fish. Cut away most of the belly to make nice back pieces, 7–10 cm long. Bring the water and salt to the boil. Leave to cool.

Pour the brine over the fish and refrigerate over-night. Remove the fish from the liquid and wipe it dry in a tea towel. Place double sheets of plastic foil on the worktop. Roll up the fish in the plastic foil and tie the ends. Transfer to the freezer and freeze thoroughly.

Set the oven to 50 °C. Remove the fish from the freezer and take off the plastic foil. Smoke the frozen pike-perch with alder chips in a smoker box for 3–5 min-utes. Remove the fish and chill it. Roll it up in plastic foil again and cook it in the oven with steam or in a bain-marie until the inner temperature reaches 48 °C. Chill after cooking and slice before serving.

Crab brawn

10–12 servings

450 g crab meat
5 sheets of gelatine
3 dl mussel stock
1 lemon grass
2 dill stalks

▶ Hastily chop the crab meat and squeeze out the moisture.

Soak the sheets of gelatine in cold water for about 5 minutes. Bring the mussel stock, the lemon grass (parted) and the dill stalks to the boil. Remove the gelatine and melt it in the stock. Leave for about 10 minutes. Strain the liquid. Line a terrine mould, about

3 x 15 cm, with plastic foil; this will be made easier if you grease the mould with a little oil first. Mix the mussel stock and crab meat together. Pour the mixture into the terrine mould. Cover with plastic foil and refrigerate at least 6 hours to set. Slice before serving.

Whitefish roe on potato cakes, soured cream and red onion

10 servings
2 large, firm potatoes
salt
pepper
3 tbsp butter
2 dl whitefish roe
1 dl crème fraîche
1 small red onion, chopped fine
small flowers of crown dill
black pepper

► Peel the potatoes and grate them on the medium side of the grater. Put them in a tea towel and squeeze out all the moisture. Season with salt and pepper. Shape the potatoes into small pucks and fry them in butter for about 4 or 5 minutes on each side until they are golden brown. Serve them on a dish, garnished with crème fraîche, whitefish roe, red onion and dill flower and a slight twist of the (black) peppermill.

Smoked eel with scrambled egg

10 servings
4 eggs
½ dl Dijon mustard
2 dl milk
40 g butter, in cubes
salt
Accompaniment:
200 g flat-smoked eel

► Break the eggs and mix them with the mustard, milk and butter saucepan. Heat over a low flame, whisking continuously, until the mixture is smooth and creamy. Remove from the heat and add a little salt.

Skin the eel and cut it into small cubes. Put the scrambled egg into cups or ramekins and top it with the eel.

Silver-eel

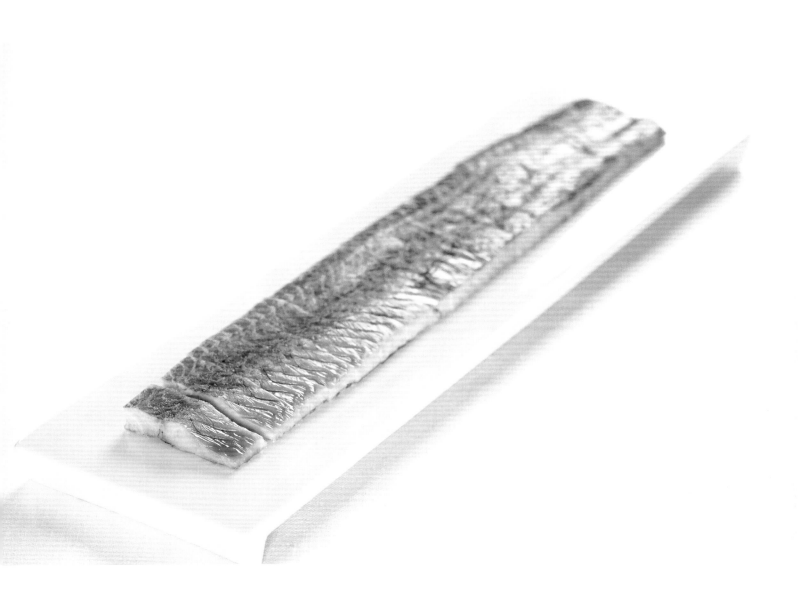

Flat-smoked eel

The saying goes that a genuine eel feast (*ålagille*) is only to be had in an eel fisher's boathouse by the sea between Åhus and Yngsjö. At least four different renderings are called for, such as eel soup and eel smoked, fried and boiled.

Salmon poached in fennel

10–20 servings

500 g fresh filet of salmon –
the middle part, with the skin
removed
Poaching liquid:
½ carrot
½ leek, only the white part
½ stalk of celery
¼ fennel bulb
1 shallot
5 dl water
1½ dl dry white wine
1 tbsp white wine vinegar
1 bay leaf
1 parsley stalk
½ tbsp fennel seeds
½ orange, grated zest of
8 white peppercorns

▶ Set the oven to 100 °C. Cut
the salmon into small cubes.
Do the same with all the
vegetables for the poaching
liquid. Bring the water, wine,
vinegar, vegetables and
spices to the boil and simmer
for about 5 minutes. Put the
cubes of salmon into a dish
with a rim at least 3 cm high
and pour the warm liquid
over them. Leave in the oven
for 5 minutes, then leave the
salmon to cool in the liquid.
Put the dish in the fridge
when the liquid has cooled.
The salmon can be served
directly, but it will keep for
about 2 days in the liquid.

Remove it from the poaching
liquid before serving.

Crayfish terrine
10–20 servings
500 g crayfish tails, peeled
30 g dill
4½ sheets of gelatine
2½ dl shellfish stock
1 tsp champagne vinegar
sea salt
► Squeeze the crayfish in a tea towel, to extract the moisture, and clean and trim them. Put dill into boiling water, remove it and chill it in iced water. Dry, pluck and chop the dill.

Soak the sheets of gelatine in cold water for about 5 minutes. Warm the shellfish stock. Remove the sheets of gelatine from the water and melt them in the stock. Add vinegar and salt to taste. Test for setting (the jelly) and flavour. Cool to 30 ˚C.

Line the inside of a terrine mould with plastic foil. Mix the crayfish with dill and the shellfish stock and transfer to the terrine mould, heaping slightly. Press the crayfish down with a weight and put them in the fridge to ripen and set.

Turn out the terrine and slice it. This will be easiest if the plastic is still on and the knife has been warmed slightly.

Boiling crayfish
10–20 servings
1 kg live crayfish
3 litres of water
about 1 dl coarse salt
5 sugar lumps
1 bottle of beer (33 cl)
1 onion, sliced
30 dill crowns
► Mix the water, salt, lumps, beer, onion and about 10 dill crowns together in a large saucepan. Boil for about 15 minutes. Remove the dill. Rinse the crayfish in cold water and put them to drain. Transfer them to the boiling liquid and add fresh dill crowns. Take care to keep the crayfish under the surface and make sure the water is boiling properly. Boil the crayfish for about 6 minutes. Remove them and put them in jars together with dill crowns. Pour the cooking liquid over them and cool both crayfish and cooking liquid rapidly. Leave the crayfish in the liquid for at least 2 days, to give them time to ripen.

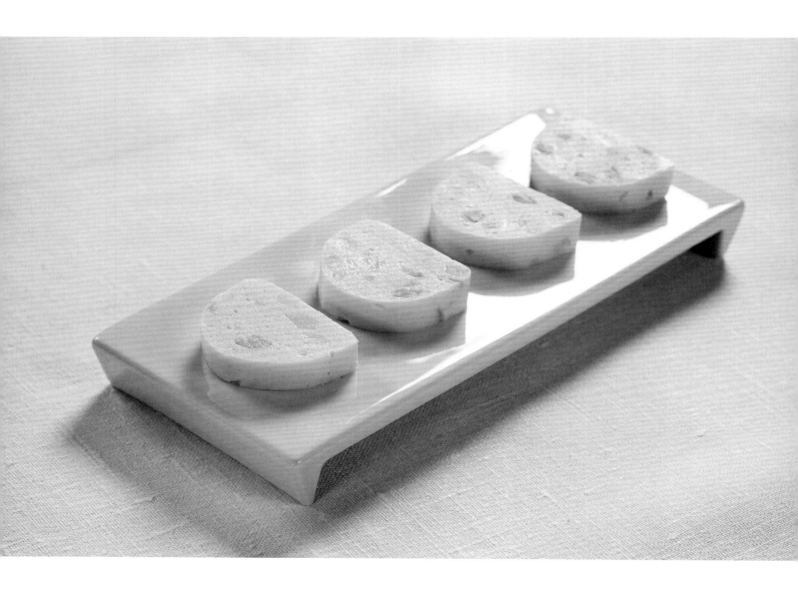

Fish pâté with coquille St Jacques and salmon

10–20 servings

250 g filet of pike or pike-
perch
about 1 tsp salt
2½ dl whipping cream
½ white of egg
100 g coquilles St Jacques,
cut in cubes
50 g cold-smoked salmon,
cut in cubes

► Set the oven to 75 °C. Cut the fish in pieces and put them in the freezer. Remove when semi-frozen and mix with salt in a food processor. Add the cream in a thin jet with the machine still run-ning. Store in a cold place. Beat the white of egg to a stiff foam and mix it with the coquilles St Jacques and salmon. Fold this into the pâté mixture. Line an oblong tin, about 20 x 4 cm, with plastic foil. Press the fish mixture down into the tin and make sure there are no air bubbles; tap the tin on the worktop to prevent this happening. Fold the plastic foil over and make sure it fits closely. Bake the pâté for 30–45 minutes, depend-ing on the size of the tin, until the inner temperature reaches 68–70 °C. Leave to cool and refrigerate, under pressure, till next day.

Char terrine

10–20 servings

1 kg char filets, with skin and
bones removed
½ dl caster sugar
½ dl salt
8–10 white peppercorns,
crushed
6 sheets of gelatine
3 dl dry white wine
2 dl water

► Mix the sugar, salt and
white peppercorns together.
Rub the mixture into the
filets. Leave to cure for about
30 minutes at room temperature, covered with plastic foil
or else in a plastic bag. Rinse
the filets quickly and wipe
them dry. Soak the sheets
of gelatine in cold water
for about 5 minutes. Bring

the wine and water to the
boil. Transfer the sheets of
gelatine to this mixture and
melt them. Let the jelly liquid
cool to about 30 °C. Line
the inside of an oblong tin
or mould, about 20 x 4 cm,
with the plastic foil. Dip the
char filets in the jelly liquid
and place them overlapping
in the mould. Fill the mould

slightly heaped. Put a weight
on top, to press down on the
fish. Put in the freezer for at
least 2 days. Thaw the fish
slowly in the fridge. Cut the
terrine into serving portions.
This is easiest when the terrine is cold or semi-frozen.

Mr Mollberg's savoury

10 servings
300 g shelled shrimps
100 g cold-smoked salmon, diced
1½ tbsp salted cucumber, diced
1½ tbsp chopped apple
1½ tbsp chopped red onion
1 tbsp grated horseradish
1 tbsp Swedish mustard
2 tbsp mayonnaise
10 pie casings (see recipe p. 51)
Accessories:
10 egg yolks, quails' eggs preferably
Garnish:
herbs, e.g. dill, chives, parsley and chervil
► Chop the shrimps hastily and mix with the smoked salmon. Fold in the salted cucumber, apple, red onion and grated horseradish. Carefully stir in the mustard and mayonnaise. Serve with a topping of egg yolk and herbs.

Skagen shrimps in a pie

10 servings
250 g peeled shrimps
1 dl mayonnaise
2 tbsp Dijon mustard
1 tbsp champagne vinegar
2 tbsp grated horseradish
10 pie casings (see recipe p. 51)
Garnish:
80 g bleak roe
sprigs of dill
► Wipe the shrimps dry in kitchen tissue. Mix the mayonnaise, Dijon mustard, vinegar and horseradish. For a milder Skagen salad, cut back on the Dijon mustard and horseradish. Mix the sauce, a little at a time, with the shrimps to the desired consistency. Put the Skagen salad into the ramekins and top with bleak roe and a sprig of dill when serving.

Den Gyldene Freden's classic gentleman's savoury

10 servings
6 eggs
5 Swedish anchovy filets
½ red onion, peeled
1 tbsp chopped chives
1 tbsp chopped dill
1 egg yolk
2 tbsp caviar, e.g. Swedish Kalles kaviar
10 pie casings (see recipe p. 51)
or bits of *kavring* rye bread
Accompaniment:
10 egg yolks, from quails' eggs if possible
chives
black pepper
► Put the eggs in boiling water and boil them for about 12 minutes until they are hard boiled. Chill them and shell them. Chop the egg, anchovy and red onion and mix them with the chives and dill. Fold the egg yolk and caviar into the savoury, stirring carefully so as not to mash the egg or anchovy. Serve in a pie crust or on *kavring* rye bread, with an egg yolk on top.

Matjes herring torte

10–20 servings
300 g *kavring* rye bread
100 g melted butter
Filling:
300 g matjes herring
1 small red onion, peeled
1 tbsp chopped chives
1 tbsp chopped dill
2 sheets of gelatine
2½ dl crème fraîche
125 g green cheese

▶ Run the *kavring* in the food processor with melted butter so it crumbles. Line a tin, about 20 x 4 cm, with plastic foil. Spread the crumbs over the bottom of the tin and press them smooth. Put the tin in the fridge until this has set. Chop the matjes herring and red onion and mix them with the herbs. Soak the sheets of gelatine in cold water for about 5 minutes. Mix the crème fraîche and green cheese with a stick blender. Heat ¼ of this mixture in a saucepan. Remove the sheets of gelatine from the water and melt them in the mixture. Stir this and the remaining crème fraîche together. Fold in the matjes herring and herbs in half of the cheese mixture and scoop into the tin. Smooth the surface. Pour the rest of the cheese mixture on top, smooth it out and put the torte in the fridge for about 3 hours to set. Cut the terrine into serving portions with a dry, warm knife.

Potato and matjes herring terrine

10–20 servings
500 g potato
75 g butter, at room temperature
3 tbsp crème fraîche
1 tbsp olive oil
2 tsp coarse Dijon mustard
salt
pepper
2 sheets of gelatine
1½ dl dry white wine
150 g matjes herring
15 leaves of flat-leafed parsley

▶ Boil the potatoes till they are soft. Drain away the water, put the lid back on the saucepan and leave for a while, for the steam to finish the job. Peel the potatoes and crush them hastily, adding knobs of butter, crème fraîche, olive oil and mustard. Stir carefully until everything has melted. Add salt and pepper to taste. Leave to cool a little.

Soak the sheets of gelatine in cold water for about 5 minutes. Bring the wine to the boil. Remove the gelatine from the water and melt it in the warm wine.

Cut the matjes herring filets into cubes and put them on kitchen tissue to dry. Line the inside of a terrine mould with plastic foil. Cover the bottom with a layer of potato, smoothing it out. Brush with the wine-and-jelly mixture and put the herring on top. Brush again with the wine-and-jelly mixture and put parsley leaves on top. Brush again. Cover with a layer of potato. Fold the plastic foil over the terrine and put a weight on top. Refrigerate overnight. Be careful when slicing the terrine, so it doesn't disintegrate.

Buckling casserole
10–12 servings
6 buckling filets
1 dl onion
1 dl chopped salted cucumber
1 dl chopped capers
2 tbsp chives, chopped
1 dl Swedish mustard-dill
sauce ("head waiter's sauce"),
(see recipes p. 237)
► Skin the filets and break
them up. Arrange them on a
serving dish with onion, salted
cucumber, capers and chives
lined up on top of them. Pour
the sauce over the vegetables
in thin streaks.

Poached perch

10–20 servings

500 g perch filets with the skin removed

Poaching liquid:

1 small shallot
50 g celeriac
1 small carrot
1 small yellow carrot
1 litre water
1 tbsp salt
1 tsp pressed lemon
4 white peppercorns
1 bay leaf
4 dill stalks

► Set the oven to 100 °C. Remove all bones and cut the fish into oblong pieces. Put the filets in a saucepan. Peel and slice the shallot. Peel and dice the celeriac. Peel the carrots and slice them crosswise. Bring the water, salt, lemon, spices and vegetables to the boil. Pour the warm liquid over the perch and put it in the oven for 5–7 minutes. Leave it to cool in the liquid. Arrange the perch on a serving dish and garnish with the vegetables before serving. The perch will keep for 2 days in the liquid if stored in the fridge.

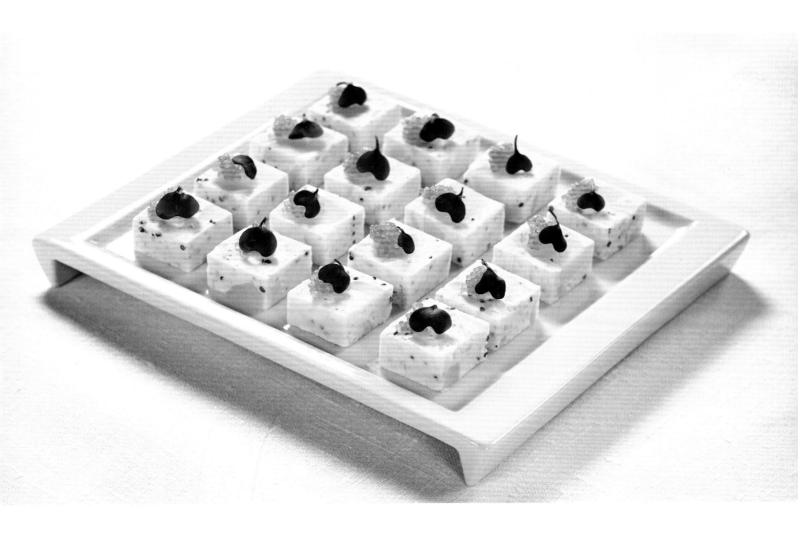

Potato terrine with bleak roe

10 servings

200 g peeled potatoes
2 sheets of gelatine
1 dl crème fraîche
1 tbsp coarse cider vinegar
mustard
about ½ tsp salt
Accompaniments:
50 g bleak roe
soured cream (*gräddfil*)
small plucked herb leaves

► Boil the potatoes. Put the sheets of gelatine to soak in cold water for about 5 minutes. Heat the crème fraîche. Remove the sheets of gelatine and melt them in the crème fraîche. Crush the potatoes hastily and mix them with the crème fraîche, mustard and salt. Cover a small terrine mould, 3x15 cm, with plastic foil and pour the potato mixture into it. Cover with plastic foil and put a weight on top. Refrigerate for at least 6 hours. Cut the potato terrine in pieces. Garnish with bleak roe, soured cream (*gräddfil*) and leaves.

Cold-smoked salmon

10–12 servings

500 g loin of salmon (the thickest part of the back)

9½ dl water

50 g salt

3 dl alder chips

► Clean the salmon, removing
all skin and bones. Bring salt
water to the boil and leave to
cool. Pour this over the salmon
and refrigerate overnight.
Remove the salmon and wipe
it dry in a tea towel. Arrange
double sheets of plastic foil on
the worktop. Roll up the salmon in the plastic foil and tie the
ends. Put it in the freezer and
freeze it all the way through.

   Set the oven to 38 °C.
Remove the salmon from the
freezer and take off the plastic.
Smoke the salmon with alder
chips in a smoker box for 3–5
minutes. It is important for
the salmon to be smoked in
the frozen state. Remove the
salmon. Roll it up in plastic foil
again and bake it in the oven
with steam or a bain-marie for
about 30 minutes, till the inner
temperature reaches 32 °C.
Cool the salmon again. Slice
thinly before serving.

Warm-smoked salmon
10–12 servings
500 g loin of salmon (the thickest part of the back)
9½ dl water
50 g salt
3 dl alder chips
1 bunch of thyme
4 bay leaves
1 tbsp crushed caraway
► Day 1: Trim the salmon and cut away the skin. Bring salt water to the boil and leave to cool. Put in the salmon and refrigerate overnight. Day 2: Remove the salmon and wipe it with kitchen tissue. Cut it into pieces measuring about 3 x 3 cm. Roll these in plastic foil and put them in the freezer till they are barely frozen. Remove from the freezer, take off the plastic.

Fill a plastic-coated frying pan with alder chips, thyme, bay leaves and caraway. Place the cubes of fish on a wire rack in the cold oven. Heat the frying pan on the hob until smoke starts coming from the chips. Cover and leave for another minute. Now put the frying pan on the floor of the oven, remove the lid and close the oven front. Leave for about 5 minutes. Remove the salmon and leave it to thaw at room temperature on a wire rack. Set the oven to 250 °C. Put in the salmon and bake it in the middle of the oven for 4–6 minutes. Remove and put to cool.

Salmon mousse
10–12 servings
300 g boiled salmon
200 warm-smoked salmon
2 dl white wine sauce
6 dl whipping cream
5 sheets of gelatine
4 cl dry white wine
4 cl brandy
salt
white pepper
► Mix the fish and white wine sauce with a stick blender or in the food processor. Sieve the farce. Whisk the cream lightly. Soak the sheets of gelatine in cold water for about 5 minutes. Heat the wine and brandy in a saucepan and melt the sheets of gelatine in this mixture. Fold the gelatine mixture into the salmon mixture. Carefully fold in the cream. Season with salt and pepper. Pour the mixture into a terrine mould, 20 x 5 cm, lined with plastic foil. Store the terrine cold for at least 8 hours, to give it time to set before slicing.

White wine sauce
10–20 servings
3½ dl fish stock
1½ dl Noilly Prat
1½ dl dry white wine
1 shallot
½ leek, the white part
4 dl whipping cream
1 tsp pressed lemon
1–2 pinches of salt
1 tbsp Maizena corn starch
► Mix the fish stock, Noilly Prat and wine in a saucepan. Peel the onion and chop small. Trim the leek and chop small. Add the onion and leek to the saucepan and simmer till reduced by half. Strain the stock through a fine sieve. Pour in the cream and bring to the boil. Add lemon and salt to taste. Thicken the sauce with corn starch dissolved in a little cold water. Strain the sauce and serve it directly, or else store it in the fridge.

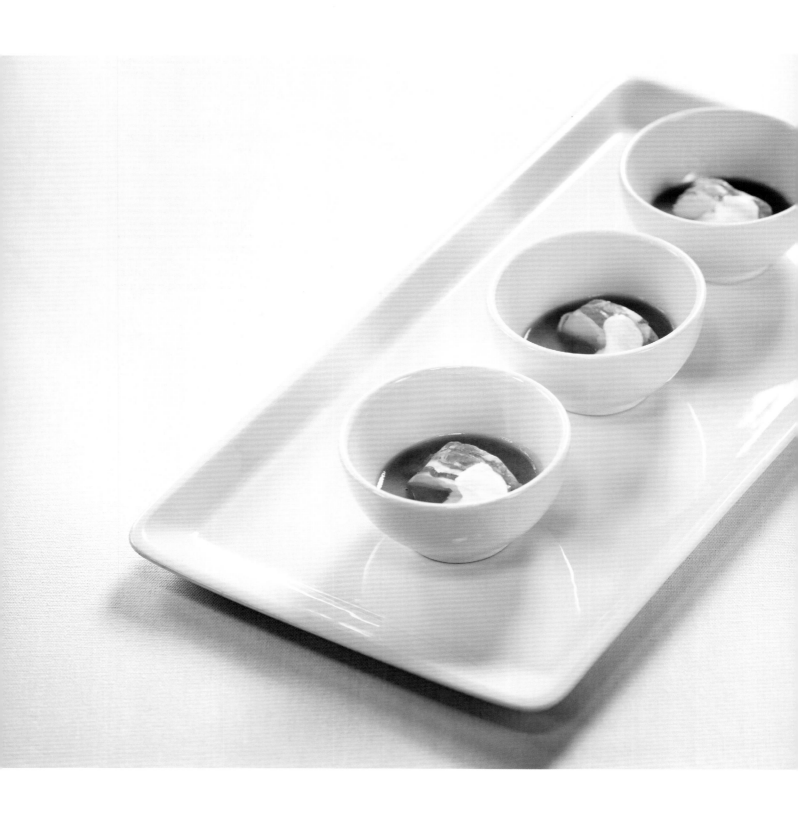

Green pea soup with lobster
Serve hot or cold, as preferred
10 servings
1 shallot, chopped
2 tbsp butter
4 dl vegetable stock
2 dl green peas (fresh-frozen
will do fine)
salt
pepper
Garnish:
1 dl whipping cream
1–2 tsp pressed lemon juice
10 pcs boiled lobster tail
► Sauté the onion in butter in
a saucepan. Pour on the stock
and bring to the boil. Add the
peas and bring quickly to the
boil again. Run this mixture to
a soup. Add salt and pepper
to taste.

Beat the cream lightly, adding lemon juice to taste. Pour
the soup into small cups. Put
a piece of lobster in each and
garnish with the cream.

Cold cuts

This round consist of meat, fresh and cured, served cold and sliced. Here you will find rabbit sausage, wild boar, brawn, pasties, reindeer pâté, breast of duck, venison of roe deer, lamb, pork and a good deal more besides.

During the infancy of the smörgåsbord, it was pork that was served. Veal and game were added later. Nothing was allowed to be wasted when livestock were slaughtered. But the smörgåsbord, like everything else, is changing and, nowadays, to make this round less of an obstacle course, it also includes lighter meat dishes such as chicken, turkey and duck.

Rustic calf's liver paste

10–20 servings
175 g calf's liver
250 g diced ribs of pork or fresh side pork
75 g lard
½ red onion, chopped small
1 tbsp butter
½ tsp marjoram
½ tsp thyme
3 Swedish anchovy filets
1¼ dl white flour
3 dl whipping cream
2 eggs
1 tbsp golden syrup
about 1 tsp salt
ground white pepper

► Trim the liver, removing all sinews and membranes. Coarse-grind the liver, ribs or side pork and lard. Fry the onion with the marjoram and thyme in butter till soft. Leave to cool. Chop the Swedish anchovy. Beat the sifted flour and whipping cream together into a smooth batter. Fold in the minced meat together with the eggs and syrup. It is important that all the ingredients should be cold. Add the Swedish anchovy and onion. Season with salt and pepper. Test a sample of the mixture to check the seasoning. Remember that liver paste does not have quite such a strong flavour when served cold. Line an oven-proof dish (1½–2 litres) with baking paper. This will stick better if you apply rapeseed oil to the edges.

Set the oven to 125 °C. Bake for about 1 hour, till the temperature is 72 °C. The mixture must have set completely and the juices must run clear when you test with a skewer. Remove and leave to cool in the dish. Store in the fridge with a weight on top for compression.

Fine liver paste

10–20 servings
300 g calf's liver
about 2½ dl milk
1 small onion, chopped fine
1 tbsp butter
100 g ribs of pork
50 g chicken mince
25 g Swedish anchovy filets
1 pinch of ground allspice
1 tsp salt
1 pinch of nitrite salt or salt-petre
1 tsp marjoram
1 egg

► Day 1: Trim the liver, removing all sinews and membranes, and cut up small. Put the pieces in a bowl and cover with milk. Store in the fridge for 24 hours.

Day 2: Set the oven to 100 °C. Remove the liver from the milk and wipe it dry. Fry the onion in butter till soft. Put the ribs of pork, chicken mince, liver, onion and Swedish anchovy twice through the meat grinder, using the finest disc. Stir in the spices. Run the mixture in a food processor and add the egg. Fry a sample. Cover a small terrine mould, 3 x 20 cm, with plastic foil. Pour in the farce and bake in a bain-marie till the inner temperature reaches 68–70 °C. Leave to cool in the mould.

Liver paste in lard

15–20 servings
100 g shallot
100 g spring onion
1 tbsp butter
200 g toast with the crusts removed
4 eggs
600 g mild-flavoured pig's liver
10 g dried marjoram
salt
black pepper
1 g nitrite salt
300 g lardo or lard, in thin slices

► Peel and chop the onion. Chop the spring onion. Sauté the onion in butter. Cut the bread in cubes and mix with the eggs. Cut the liver in cubes and mix with the bread mixture, marjoram, salt, pepper and nitrite. Add the onion and refrigerate for about 3 hours. Put everything through the mincer, using the finest disc. Fry a sample, to check the seasoning. Sieve the mixture, for maximum smoothness.

Set the oven to 100 °C. Line a small terrine mould, 3 x 15 cm, with plastic foil and then with thin slices of lard. Fill it with the mixture and tap it on the table to dispose of any air pockets. Cover with plastic foil and bake in the oven with 100% steam till the inner temperature reaches 70 °C. Refrigerate for at least 12 hours, with a weight on top, before serving.

Tea–smoked venison (roe deer)

Keep a lid and a damp tea towel handy when smoking the venison.

15–20 servings

1 inner filet of (roe deer) venison, about 400 g
Pickling brine:
1 litre water
40 g salt
25 g caster sugar
Smoking:
2 dl long grain rice
2 dl caster sugar
2 tea bags, e.g. Earl Grey

► Day 1: Mix the water, salt and sugar together. Bring to the boil and leave to cool. Trim the venison, removing all sinews. Put it into the brine mixture and leave in the fridge for 24 hours.

Day 2: Dry the meat, roll it up in plastic and aluminium foil, shaping it like a Christmas cracker. Put it in the freezer for at least 12 hours.

Cover the bottom of an old saucepan with aluminium foil. Cut the tea bags open. Mix all the ingredients for smoking together and spread them evenly on the foil. Put a wire rack or a tin, about 5 cm high, into the saucepan. Remove the plastic and aluminium foil from the frozen meat and place the meat on the rack in the saucepan. Heat the saucepan with the lid on, to make things really smoky for the rice mixture. Remove the saucepan from the heat when it is full of smoke and put a tea towel over the lid to help prevent it leaking. (It is important for the lid to fit closely; the rice mixture will then retain the heat.) Leave the saucepan covered for 10–15 minutes.

Set the oven to 100 °C. Transfer the meat to an oven-proof dish and put it in the oven. Roast it till the inner temperature reaches 58–60 °C, then put it to cool.

Venison pastrami

15–20 servings

500 g inner filet of venison (reindeer)
Pickling brine:
9 ½ dl water
50 g salt
Spices:
2 tbsp coriander seeds, crushed
2 tbsp black pepper, crushed

► Day 1: Mix the water and salt together. Bring to the boil and leave to cool. Put the meat in the brine and store in the fridge overnight.

Day 2: Set the oven to 100 °C. Remove the meat and wipe it dry. Roll it in the crushed spices and place it on a sheet of aluminium foil folded double. Twist and shape into a Christmas cracker. Roast it for 10–12 minutes, till the inner temperature reaches 58–60 °C. Remove the meat from the oven, discard the foil and brown the meat quickly in a hot frying pan. Leave to cool. Serve thinly sliced.

Suovas tartar

15–20 servings

500 g suovas (cold-smoked inner filet of reindeer)
1 small red onion
½ clove of garlic
5 cornichons
1 sardelle (anchovy) filet
1½ tbsp capers
1 tbsp shredded parsley
1 tbsp olive oil
½ tsp sea salt
2 tbsp Dijon mustard
1 tbsp mayonnaise
1 dl plucked herbs
grated horseradish
diced beetroot

► Cut the suovas into small cubes. Peel and chop the onion and garlic. Chop the cornichons. Shred the sardelle filet. Mix the meat with red onion, garlic, cornichons, sardelle, capers, parsley and olive oil. Fold in the salt, mustard and mayonnaise. Transfer the mixture to a small bowl, about 3 x 10 cm, coated with plastic foil and tip out onto a serving dish. Garnish with herbs, grated horseradish and diced beetroot.

Brawn of home-killed pork

10–20 servings

750 g pig's cheek with the rind still on
250 g shoulder of pork
1 pig's trotter, divided
1 salted pig's tongue
4 litres water
225 g sea salt
125 g caster sugar
50 g nitrite salt
Day 2:
5 black peppercorns
3 bay leaves
3 sprigs of thyme
2 parsley stalks
1 tbsp fresh ginger, sliced
2 cloves of garlic, sliced
1 onion, sliced

1 carrot, peeled and sliced
2 dl dry white wine
3–4 sheets of gelatine
200 g lard, in thin slices

► Day 1: Boil the pickling brine ingredients together and leave to cool. Put the cheek, shoulder of pork and pig's trotter into the pickling brine and leave them there for 12 or 16 hours in the fridge.

Day 2: Remove the meat from the pickling brine and rinse quickly under the cold tap together with the pig's tongue. Bring the water to the boil. Put in all the meat and bring to the boil. Remove the meat and wipe it dry before

putting it into another saucepan. Add the spices and vegetables, pour on enough wine and water to cover. Bring to the boil and skim. Simmer gently for about 3 hours, until the meat is really tender. Soak the sheets of gelatine in cold water for 5 minutes. Remove the meat and strain the stock. Pull the skin off the tongue. Divide the tongue and meat into large pieces and cover these with foil to keep them warm. Heat 5 dl of the stock. Remove the sheets of gelatine from the water and melt them in the warm stock.

Dip the lard quickly in sim-

mering water. Put to cool in ice water. Line the inside of a terrine mould, 4 x 4 x 25 cm, with plastic foil. Cover the mould with the sliced lard, leaving enough hanging over the edges to cover the top part of the brawn.

Fold the warm pieces of tongue and meat into the gelatine liquid. Arrange them attractively in the terrine mould, heaping them slightly. Fold the lard over, followed by the plastic foil. Store in the fridge with a weight on top.
Leave to cool overnight.

Veal brawn

15–20 servings

2 kg salted loin of veal
2 tbsp distilled vinegar (*ättika*, 12% strength)
2 litres water
2 bay leaves
5 white peppercorns
6 allspice corns
4 stalks of thyme
3 stalks of parsley
½ leek, peeled and sliced
1 carrot
2 cm fresh ginger
2 gelatine sheets
juice of 1 lemon
2 tsp coarse French mustard

► Put the veal in a cooking pot together with 1 tbsp distilled vinegar and enough water to cover. Bring to the boil and then pour off the water. Now do the same once more.

Put the veal into a cooking pot with the spices and vegetables. Simmer gently for about 3 hours, until the meat starts coming away from the bone or dissolves into threads. Remove the meat and leave it to cool slightly. Strain the stock and save 4 dl for later. Soak the sheets of gelatine in cold water for about 5 minutes. Remove them and melt them in the stock. Add the lemon juice. Pick the meat from the bones and dice it. Mix it with a little of the stock and the mustard. Test the seasoning. Put the meat into plastic-lined, slightly rounded terrine moulds, about 20 cm long, and cover with the rest of the liquid. Put in the fridge under pressure to set.

Tongue in aspic

15–20 servings

1 salted tongue
1 carrot, orange or yellow
1 celery stalk
½ leek (the white part)
water
4–5 dried juniper berries
1 bay leaf
6 white peppercorns
1 tbsp shredded flat-leafed parsley
4 sheets of gelatine

► Rinse the calf's tongue in running cold water for about 5 minutes. Peel the carrot. Trim the celery and leek. Cut up the vegetables. Put the tongue in a saucepan together with the vegetables and spices. Pour on enough water to cover. Bring to the boil, cover and simmer for about 3 hours, skimming at regular intervals. Remove the tongue and transfer to a bowl. Cover it with plastic foil, to keep the surface from drying. Leave to cool slightly. Strain off the liquid and reserve 4 dl of the stock and the carrot. Soak the sheets of gelatine in cold water for about 5 minutes. Remove the skin from the tongue while it is still warm. Dice it. Remove the sheets of gelatine and melt them in 4 dl of the strained stock. Crush the carrot with a fork and mix it with the tongue and stock. Pour into a plastic-lined mould, about 1 litre, and put in the fridge to set. Serve sliced.

Farmhouse terrine of wild boar

15–20 servings

400 g ribs or steak of wild boar, trimmed and with sinews etc. removed
150 g salted shoulder of pork
200 g lard
1 ½ tsp salt
½ tsp milled black pepper
2 pinches of grated nutmeg
1 bay leaf
1½ tbsp brandy
1 tbsp thyme
2 eggs
250 g boiled ham
250 g smoked side pork
50 g dried black trumpet mushrooms, soaked and squeezed dry
1 tbsp butter
50 g pistachio nuts, coarsely chopped
200 g thinly sliced lard

► Dice the ribs, shoulder of pork and lard. Mix thoroughly with the salt, pepper, nutmeg, bay leaf, brandy and thyme. Store in the fridge overnight. Put the marinated meat through the mincer, using the coarsest disc, and mix in the eggs. Set the oven to 100 ℃. Dice the ham and side pork. Fry the black trumpet mushrooms in butter. Mix the ham, side pork, mushrooms and pistachio nuts with the farce. Line a tin, of about 1½ litres capacity, with plastic foil. Cover the bottom and sides with slices of lard, and let them hang over the sides. Fill the tin with farce and fold over the slices of lard. Cover with aluminium foil folded double.

Bake in the oven for 1½–2 hours, till the inner temperature reaches 70 °C. Leave to cool. Store in the fridge with a weight on top, at least overnight.

Reindeer pâté

15–20 servings

300 g "roast beef" of reindeer venison
300 g ribs of pork
150 g lard
1½ dl red port
15 crushed juniper berries
1 tsp dried thyme
15 g dried black trumpet mushrooms or other mushrooms
2 shallots
2 tbsp butter
3 slices of dry white bread
1–2 dl milk
2 packets bacon (2 x 140 g)
1 egg
30 g pistachio nuts, coarsely chopped
1½ tsp salt
½ tsp nitrite salt
½ tsp milled white pepper
150 g inner filet of (reindeer) venison

► Day 1: Cut up the "roast beef", ribs and lard. Mix with the port, juniper berries and thyme. Marinate the meat and lard in the fridge for 12 hours.

Day 2: Soak the dried mushrooms in water for about 30 minutes. Squeeze dry and chop coarsely. Peel the shallots and chop small. Sauté the onion and mushroom in butter. Leave to cool. Dice the bread and pour on just enough milk to cover. Leave it to swell. Set the oven to 100 °C. Line a small rounded terrine mould, about 20 cm, with bacon, and let the rashers hang over the sides. Pour off and reserve the port from the meat. Put the marinated meat and spices together with the bread through the mincer, using the finest disc. Stir the meat, eggs, onion, mushrooms, pistachio nuts and port together, adding milk if necessary until you

have a good consistency. Season with salt and pepper. Fry a sample to check the seasoning. Remember that the pâté will be less strongly flavoured when served cold. Spread the farce and inner filet in the mould, fold the bacon over and cover with baking paper and aluminium foil. Bake in a bain-marie for about 1-1½ hours, until the inner temperature reaches 68–70 °C. Remove from the oven and put to cool under pressure in the fridge.

Spiced breast of duck
15–20 servings
2 breasts of duck
25 g sea salt
¼ tsp whole black peppercorns
4 star anises
¼ tsp coriander seeds
grated zest of 1 orange
grated zest of 1 lemon
► Day 1: Trim the breasts, removing all sinews. Leave the skin on and score it with little squares. Crush the spices in a mortar together with the orange and lemon zest. Cover the breasts with the mixture and put them on a plate, fatty side downwards. Cover with plastic foil and store in the fridge for 24 hours.

Day 2: Get out the breasts and turn them over. Refrigerate for another 24 hours.

Day 3: Set the oven to 100 °C. Get out the breasts and wipe them dry. Brown them golden on the skin side in a moderately hot frying pan. Turn them over and fry for about 1 minute on the meaty side. Transfer to the oven and roast until the inner temperature reaches 60 °C. Put them to cool. Serve thinly sliced.

Roll-up of corn-fed chicken
20–30 servings
8 filets of corn-fed chicken
about 1 tsp salt
1 dl whipping cream
1 egg
1 tbsp chopped parsley
1 tsp chopped sage
100 g boiled ham, diced
salt
white pepper

► Set the oven to 100 °C. Put the chicken filets on a chopping board. Remove the piece on the inside of the filet (the inner filet). Make an incision in each filet and fold out the breast to make it twice as large. Run the inner fillets and salt to a smooth mixture in the food processor and while it is running add a thin jet of cream. Add the egg. Remove the farce and fold in the herbs and ham. Season with salt and pepper. Micro a small dob of the chicken farce and check the seasoning.

Put a sheet of aluminium foil, folded double, on the worktop. Arrange the chicken filets in a rectangle along the near side of it, slightly overlapping. Deposit a string of the farce along the lower part of the chicken. Roll up firmly, twisting to make a Christmas cracker. Take care the aluminium foil doesn't split, though. Roast on a baking tray in the oven for about 50 minutes, till the inner temperature is 68 °C. Leave to cool. Serve thinly sliced.

Collared brawn with juniper berries

15–20 servings

1 kg salted side pork
1 dl chopped pistachio nuts
1 tbsp crushed juniper berries
1 tsp crushed allspice corns

► Set the oven to 100 °C. Trim the meat smooth. Save the trimmings till later. Cut a slit down the middle of the meat and fold the meat outwards to make it twice as large. Beat it thin, sandwiched between two plastic bags, with a heavy saucepan.

Dice the trimmings small or give them a short blast of the food processor. Mix them with the pistachio nuts, juniper berries and allspice.

Spread this filling on the pork and roll up tight. Place the roll of pork on the bottom half of a double sheet of aluminium foil and roll up hard like a Christmas cracker.

Insert a thermometer in the meat and roast for at least 1 hour, till the inner temperature is 68 °C. Leave to cool, then store in the fridge overnight. Serve thinly sliced.

Mock brawn

15–20 servings

1½ kg pig's cheek with the rind still on
2 pig's trotters, divided
1 salted pig's tongue
500 g shoulder of pork
4 litres water
225 g sea salt
125 g caster sugar
50 g nitrite salt

Day 2:
1 onion
2 carrots
5 allspice corns
5 black peppercorns
3 bay leaves
4 cloves
3 sprigs of thyme
2 stalks of parsley
2 dry white wine
400 g pig's rind, thinly sliced
5 sheets of gelatine

► Day 1: Boil all the pickling brine ingredients together and leave to cool. Pickle the pig's cheek, trotters and shoulder for 8–10 hours.

Day 2: Remove the meat from the brine and rinse it lightly under the tap together with the tongue. Bring plenty of water to the boil. Put in the meat and bring to the boil again. Remove the meat and dry it. Peel the onion and car-rots and cut them up. Put the meat into a new saucepan, adding the vegetables and spices. Pour on the wine and enough water to cover. Bring to the boil and skim. Cover and simmer for about 3 hours, until the meat comes away from the bones. Dip the extra rind briefly in simmering water and chill it in iced water. Line a round mixing bowl with plastic foil, followed by the rind, thinly sliced; leave the foil and slices of rind hanging over the edge, to be folded over the brawn presently.

Remove the meat and strain the stock. Reserve the black pepper and allspice corns. Divide the meat into large and small pieces. Take 5 dl of the stock. Soak the sheets of gela-tine in cold water for about 5 minutes. Heat the stock and put the sheets of gelatine to melt in it. Mix the meat and stock together. Remove the meat again and layer it neatly with the black pepper and allspice corns and a little of the stock in the terrine mould, heaping it slightly. Fold over the rind, followed by the plas-tic foil. Leave to set overnight with a weight on top.

Brawn of pig's trotters

15–20 servings

2 salted pig's trotters
1 salted loin of pork, about
1 kg
1 carrot
1 white onion
1 stalk of celery
1 clove of garlic
1 bottle of dry French cider,
33 cl
water
1 stick of cinnamon
1 star anise
6 allspice corns
6 white peppercorns
1 stalk of parsley
3 sheets of gelatine

4 dl of the stock
1 tbsp flat-leafed parsley,
sliced thin

► Rinse the pig's trotters and loin of pork in running cold water for about 10 minutes. Peel the carrot and onion and cut them up. Trim the celery and cut it up. Peel the garlic.

Put the meat in a saucepan. Pour in the cider and top up with enough water to cover the meat. Bring to the boil and skim. Add the vegetables and spices, cover and simmer for 2–3 hours, till the meat starts coming away from the bones.

Remove the meat and car-

rot. Strain the cooking liquid. Pick the meat into pieces after it has cooled. Soak the sheets of gelatine in cold water for about 5 minutes. Mash the carrot with a fork. Remove the sheets of gelatine and melt them in the warm stock. Add the picked meat, carrot and flat-leafed parsley. Remove the meat and put it into plastic-lined moulds, 4 x 20 cm, slightly heaped. Pour on the rest of the liquid.

Cover with plastic foil and put a weight on top to flatten. Store in the fridge overnight so that it sets. Serve thinly sliced.

Marinated roast beef with garlic chips

15–20 servings
600 g roast beef
½ tsp salt
½ tsp fresh-milled black pepper
1 tbsp butter
Marinade:
2 dl beer
2 tbsp honey
1 bay leaf
5 allspice corns
2 cloves
3 dl veal stock
1 tsp salt
Accessories:
1–2 whole bulbs of garlic
4 dl rapeseed oil
lamb's lettuce or purslane

► Bring all the marinade ingredients to the boil together. Leave to cool.

Trim the roast beef, removing all sinews. Truss it into a roll with roasting string. Rub it with salt and pepper. Brown it all over in butter and transfer to an oven-proof dish. Set the oven to 70 °C. Roast the beef till the inner temperature reaches 60–62 °C. Remove it from the oven and put it in the marinade for about 2 hours.

Peel the cloves of garlic and slice them thinly. Rinse them under the cold tap for 5 minutes. Wipe them dry on a tea towel. Heat the oil to 160 °C.

Sauté the garlic slices in the oil until golden. Remove and drain on kitchen tissue. Serve the roast beef with the garlic and lettuce.

Svante's spice-dredged roast beef of lamb

15–20 servings

300 g "roast beef" of lamb
Spice mixture:
2 tbsp hazel nuts, chopped small
1 tsp smoked paprika powder
1 tsp ground cumin
½ tsp dried, flaked chilli
1 tsp instant coffee powder
½ tsp fennel seeds
1 tsp salt
1 tbsp butter

► Set the oven to 100 °C. Trim the "roast beef", removing all sinews. Mix all the spices in a spice mill. Roll the meat in the mixture. Fold a sheet of aluminium foil double on the worktop and roll the meat up in it like a Christmas cracker. Roast for about 1 hour, until the inner temperature of the meat is 60 °C. Leave to cool. Unwrap the meat and brown it all over in butter in a frying pan. Leave to cool. Serve thinly sliced.

Baked Christmas ham
10 servings
1 salted ham, 2–3 kg or a
ready-cooked one
Mustard coating:
2 egg yolks
4 tbsp Swedish sweet mustard
2 slices of fresh white bread
½–1 dl dried breadcrumbs
► Set the oven to 175 °C. Wrap
the ham in aluminium foil and
place it in an oven-proof dish.
Bake till the inner temperature
reaches 68 °C, allowing 60–70
minutes per kilo of ham. Save
the pan juices for "dip in the
pot".

A precooked ham can be
grilled immediately.

Grilling:

Raise the oven temperature
to 225 °C. Mix the egg yolks
and mustard together. Run
the bread in the food processor after removing the crusts.
Add the bread to the mustard
mixture. Spread this on the
ham and sift the dried breadcrumbs over it. Grill the ham
in the middle of the oven for
10–15 minutes, turning it from
time to time for even grilling.
Watch the time, so nothing
gets burned.

Pig's tongue, salted and boiled

15–20 servings

1 salted pig's tongue
1 shallot, peeled
½ carrot, peeled
½ stalk of celery
$^1/_3$ leek, halved
1 clove of garlic, crushed
1 bay leaf
2 stalks of breckland thyme
4 allspice corns
4 black peppercorns
1 dl dry white wine

► Rinse the tongue for 5 minutes in cold water. Wipe it dry with kitchen tissue. Put it in a saucepan together with the vegetables, spices, wine and enough water to cover. Simmer gently for 3-3½ hours, skimming at regular intervals. Test with a skewer to see when it is done; it must feel soft. Remove from the liquid, leave to cool slightly and peel off the skin. Cover with plastic foil and leave to cool properly. Serve thinly sliced.

Smoked rabbit sausage

15–20 servings

100 g calf's tongue, boiled and salted
100 g side pork, boiled and salted
30 g shallot
10 g garlic
300 g rabbit meat, minced fine
225 g rabbit meat, coarse-ground
10 g parsley, shredded fine
10 g plucked leaves of thyme
10 g Szechuan pepper, crushed
5 g mixed herbs and spices – cinnamon, cloves, black pepper, yellow mustard seeds, coarse-milled
6 g salt
3 g nitrite salt
4 cl pale stock
5 metres of hog casing
For smoking:
3 dl alder chips
½ garlic
2 sprigs of rosemary
20 juniper berries

► Day 1: Cut the tongue and pork into cubes. Peel the onion and garlic and chop them up small. Mix the meat with the onion, garlic, herbs and spices. Add the salt and stock. Mix well and fry a sample. Rinse the hog casing with cold water. Stuff the casing with the farce and tie into sausages 10 cm long. Put these in the freezer overnight.

Day 2: Take the sausages out of the freezer and put them in a cold oven. Put chips into a (preferably cast-iron) frying pan lined with aluminium foil. Put in the rosemary, the cloves of garlic (cut in strips but en chemise – not peeled) and the juniper berries. Make a lid of aluminium foil. Put the frying pan on the hob with the heat turned up full. When the smoke billows copiously forth from the frying pan, put it in the oven, removing the lid and closing the front. Smoke the sausages for about 10 minutes. Remove them and set the oven to 90 °C. Steam the sausages under plastic foil till the inner temperature reaches 70 °C. Cool in the fridge overnight.

Rabbit sausage

20–25 sausages
1 kg rabbit meat
250 g veal
275 g lard
1½ tbsp salt
2½ tbsp dry white wine
2½ dl ice-cold milk
225 g white of egg
500 g lard, diced
7–10 metres hog casing
butcher's string
Spices:
5 g white pepper
10 g fennel seeds
5 g coriander seeds

► Cut the rabbit, veal and lard into small cubes. Stir the salt, wine and the spices together and mix with the meat and lard. Marinate for 12 hours.

Put everything through the mincer, using the finest disc, and then run it in a food processor, adding the milk as you go. Pass through a strainer. Transfer to a cold mixing bowl and add the remaining spices.

Beat the whites of egg and mix them with the diced lard. Fold this into the sausage mixture, taking good care that the mixture temperature never exceeds 4 °C.

Rinse the hog casings with cold water. Thread them onto a sausage funnel and stuff them with the mixture. Tie into sausages with the butcher's string. Bring lightly salted water to the boil and simmer the sausages at 72 °C for about 40 minutes. Remove the sausages from the water and chill them with ice.

Rabbit pâté

15–20 servings
500 g diced rabbit meat
200 g turkey meat
1 egg yolk
25 g mie de pain (grated white bread)
3 dl whipping cream
1 tbsp crushed ice
salt
black pepper
1 tbsp dry sherry
Pickling medium:
9½ dl water
30 g salt
20 g nitrite salt

► Day 1: Bring the water, salt and nitrite to the boil and leave to cool. Refrigerate the rabbit meat in the pickling medium overnight.

Day 2: Set the oven to 90 °C. Put the meat through the mincer twice, using the finest disc. Run the turkey meat in a food processor. Beat the egg and mie de pain together. Fold this, with the cream and crushed ice, into the farce, a little at a time. Put the farce through a sieve.

Remove the rabbit meat from the pickling medium and wipe it dry. Sauté quickly in a frying pan, without the meat changing colour. Remove and put to cool. Mix the rabbit meat into the farce and season with salt, pepper and sherry. Fry a sample to check the seasoning.

Set the oven to 100 °C. Transfer the farce to a small plastic-lined terrine mould, 4 x 20 cm. Tap it gently on the worktop to get rid of any air bubbles. Cover with plastic foil and bake in the oven till the inner temperature reaches 70 °C. Remove the terrine and put to cool in the fridge for at least 6 hours with a weight on top.

Porcini terrine

15–20 servings
200 g turkey meat
1 egg yolk
25 g mie de pain (grated white bread)
3 dl whipping cream
1 kg porcini, cleaned, trimmed and sliced
2 tbsp unsalted butter
salt
black pepper
1 dl parsley, shredded fine and blanched
1 tbsp sherry

► Put the turkey meat twice through the mincer, using the finest disc. Now run it in the food processor. Beat the egg and mie de pain together. Fold this mixture, with the cream and crushed ice, into the farce, a little at a time. Put the farce through a sieve.

Fry the mushrooms quickly in butter. Season with salt and pepper. Remove and put to cool on a tea towel. Mix the mushrooms into the farce together with the parsley and season with salt, pepper and sherry. Fry a sample. Check the flavour.

Set the oven to 90 °C. Fill a small, plastic-lined terrine mould, 4 x 20 cm, with the farce. Tap the mould lightly on the worktop to get rid of any air bubbles. Cover the mould with plastic foil and bake in the oven till the inner temperature reaches 70 °C. Put it to cool for at least 12 hours in the fridge with a weight on top.

Lard flavoured with apple and thyme

10–20 servings

500 g coarse-ground fresh side pork
1 apple
1 shallot
1 tsp plucked thyme leaves
sea salt

► Put the side pork in a saucepan. Cook on a low flame for about 2 hours until all the fat has melted. Strain off the fat and crisp-fry the meat. Peel and de-core the apple, peel the shallot and dice them both. Sauté them in a little of the fat, until they soften but without changing colour. Pour on the rest of the fat and melt. Remove from the heat and stir in the crisp-fried pieces of pork. Leave to cool, stirring at regular intervals, and add salt to taste. Transfer to a jar and serve at room temperature with bread.

Terrine of chicken legs

15–20 servings

3 tbsp salt
3 tbsp caster sugar
½ tbsp crushed white pepper
12 legs of corn-fed chicken,
boned and trimmed
250 g bacon, either a whole
piece or rashers
3 dl flat-leafed parsley, shredded and blanched

► Mix the salt, sugar and white pepper together. Rub this mixture into the chicken and leave at room temperature for 2-3 hours, covered over with plastic foil. Next, wipe the legs with kitchen tissue.

Set the oven to 100 °C. Cut the rind off the bacon and slice it thin on the broadest side in a slicer, so as to make big slices. Line a terrine mould, size 4 x 20 cm, with plastic foil, followed by the slices of bacon. Put in a close-packed layer of chicken and sprinkle with parsley. Make alternate layers of chicken and parsley, with a layer of chicken to finish off with. Cover with plastic foil and put a weight on top. Bake the terrine till the inner temperature reaches 70 °C. Put it to cool for at least 12 hours in the fridge with a weight on top.

Frank's boudin noir
20 servings
100 g meat of pig's cheek
200 g lard
100 g meat from the pig's snout
300 g pork rind
4 g coarse-milled black pepper
1 g fine-milled allspice
1 g ground cloves
½ g ground cinnamon
2 g dried marjoram
2 g vegetable stock powder
1 g dried thyme
½ g ground ginger
3 g caster sugar
1 dl beef stock
200 g pig's blood
22 g salt per kg finished mixture
5 meter hog casings

► Day 1: Cut the meat, lard and rind into cubes. Mix with all the spices and marinate overnight in the fridge.

Day 2: Mince the meat and spices fine. Mix with the stock and blood. Run this mixture in a food processor till smooth. Fry a sample. Rinse the hog casings with cold water. Stuff the mixture into the casings and tie into sausages about 15 cm long. Steam the sausages or simmer them in stock or water with vegetables and spices. Put to cool. Slice and fry or serve cold.

Black pudding
10 servings
1 litre pig's blood
7 dl milk
7 dl coarse rye flour
2 red onions, chopped small
1 dl butter, melted
1 dl golden syrup
1 tbsp salt
½ tsp ground cloves
½ tsp white pepper
1 tsp milled allspice
1 ½ tsp marjoram
100 g lard, diced
2 sharp apples, peeled and diced

► Set the oven to 175 ºC. Strain the blood through a fine or Chinese strainer. Whisk it together with the milk and rye flour. Continue whisking vigorously while adding the remaining ingredients. Stir in the lard and diced apple.

Grease a pudding basin measuring about 25 x 30 cm and fill it three-quarters full with the mixture.

Cut greaseproof paper to fit the basin. Grease it and cover with it, topping off with aluminium foil.

Place the pudding in a bain-marie and bake in the lower half of the oven for about 1 hour.

Test to see if the pudding is done: the skewer must come away easily. When ready, leave to stand for about 15 minutes.

Farmhouse pâté from home-grown pork

15–20 servings

250 g pig's liver
450 g ribs of pork
250 g lard from the pig
2 red onions
4 cloves of garlic
½ tbsp milled black pepper
½ tbsp crushed allspice
16 g salt
5 g nitrite
2 tbsp chopped parsley
1 tbsp plucked thyme
1 dl brandy
½ dl white port
1 egg
200 g thinly sliced lard, lardo or bacon

► Day 1: Cut up the meat and lard. Peel and shred the onion and garlic. Mix the meat, onion, spices, salt, nitrite, herbs, brandy and wine together in a large mixing bowl, cover with plastic foil and refrigerate overnight.

Day 2: Set the oven to 100 °C. Put everything through the mincer, using the coarse disc. The mixture must be really cold. Add the egg and fry a sample.

Line a mould, measuring about 4 x 20 cm, with plastic foil, followed by lard or bacon. Fill the mould with the farce, tapping it lightly on the worktop to shake the mixture down. Bake till the inner temperature reaches 70 °C. Remove from the oven and refrigerate overnight with a weight on top.

Kassler terrine

15–20 servings

350 g trimmed pigmeat from the ham
240 g lard
2 cloves of garlic
1 tsp fresh thyme
1 tsp fresh marjoram
2 juniper berries, fine-ground
6 g salt
3g nitrite salt
150 g *kassler* (smoked pork)
40 g pistachio nuts
20 g truffle or black trumpet mushrooms
4 cl chicken or vegetable stock
about 400 g *kassler* in one piece, the same length as the mould
slices of lard

► Day 1: Dice the pork and lard and put them in a mould. Peel the garlic and chop small. Mix the meat and lard together with the garlic, spices, salt and nitrite. Refrigerate overnight.

Day 2: Set the oven to 100 °C. Cut the *kassler* into cubes. Chop the nuts and mushrooms. Remove the meat from the fridge and put it twice through the mincer. Mix in the *kassler* cubes, nuts, truffle and stock. Fry a sample to check the seasoning. Line a terrine mould, size 4 x 20 cm, with plastic foil. Fill this half-full with the farce. Roll the *kassler* up in lard and place it in the mould. Top up with the remaining farce. Cover with plastic foil and bake in the oven with steam for about 40 minutes, till the inner temperature reaches 70 °C. Remove and refrigerate for at least 12 hours.

Smoked grouse roll

12 servings

4 breasts of grouse with the skin removed
4¾ dl water
25 g salt
3 dl alder chips
2 cloves of garlic
1 sprig of rosemary
20 juniper berries

▶ Day 1: Trim away all sinews and remove any remaining fragments of bone. Bring the salt water to the boil and leave to cool. Refrigerate the breasts of grouse in this brine overnight.

Day 2: Remove the breasts from the brine and wipe them dry on kitchen tissue. Roll them in plastic foil and then in aluminium foil. Shape the rolls like Christmas crackers, with twisted ends.

Put the rolls in the freezer and keep them there till they are thoroughly frozen. Fill a plastic-coated frying pan with alder chips, garlic, rosemary and juniper berries. Remove the plastic and aluminium foil from the rolls.

Place the breasts on a wire rack in the cold oven. Place the frying ban on a hotplate till smoke starts coming from it, then place it in the oven and close the front.

Smoke the breasts for about 5 minutes. Remove the meat from the oven and wrap it in aluminium foil to preserve its shape. Set the oven to 100 °C. Roast the breasts in the oven until the inner temperature reaches 58 °C. Remove and leave to cool. Slice and serve.

Elk venison roast

15–20 servings

1 kg of elk venison, e.g. part of the rump steak

½ litre water

1 dl salt

2 tsp caster sugar

► Remove all sinews from the meat. Roll it up in a double sheet of aluminium foil and store in the freezer till frozen solid. Set the oven to 100 °C. Roast the meat in the oven for 6–8 hours.

Bring water, salt and sugar to the boil, then leave to cool. Put in the warm meat and store in the fridge for 2–3 hours.

Pork noisettes with herb cream

4 servings or 10 for a smörgås-bord

500 g pork chops, off the bone
1 pinch of caster sugar
½ pinch of black pepper
½ lemon, grated zest
1 tbsp rapeseed oil
Herb oil:
1 dl rocket
1 dl parsley leaves
2 tbsp basil leaves
1 tbsp Dijon mustard
1 dl rapeseed oil
1 clove of garlic
1 pinch of salt

► Cut the meat into 4 chops. Rub them with salt, sugar, pepper, lemon and oil. Grill them on the grill or in a grill pan till they are done right through, with an inner temperature of 64 °C. Leave to one side.

Boil water and blanche the rocket, parsley and basil for about 20 seconds. Chill in iced water. Drain and dry well. Mix with mustard and oil and strain. Peel the clove of garlic and grate it in, adding salt to taste.

Slice the chops and pour the oil over them.

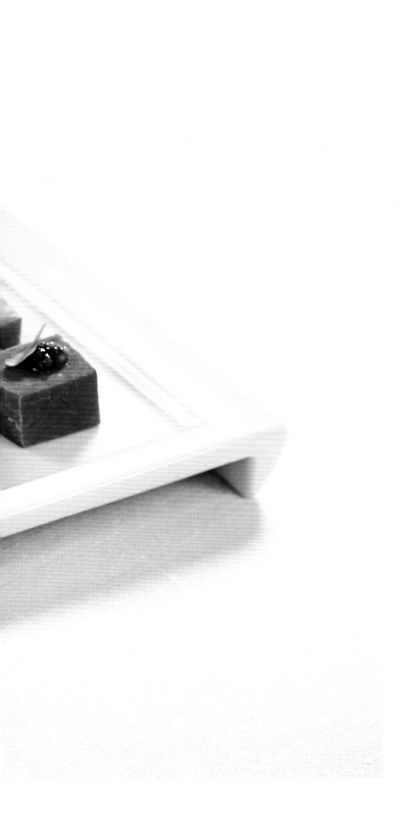

Cubes of brisket
10–12 servings
1 kg boiled salt brisket (see recipe p. 139)
Accessories:
2 tbsp coarse mustard
1 dl plucked herb leaves, freely chosen
► Boil the brisket as per the above recipe, but this time for 3 hours. Remove it and put it under pressure. Cut the meat into cubes when it is cold.
   Arrange on a serving dish and garnish with coarse mustard and leaves.

Veal olives

10–12 servings
600 g outer or inner fillet of veal, one piece
1 shallot
1 dl plucked parsley
150 g coarse-ground veal
2 anchovy (sardelle) filets
1 clove of garlic
100 g matured cheese (*präst-ost*)
salt
black pepper
1 tbsp olive oil
Garnish:
50 g matured cheese (*präst-ost*)
1 dl plucked parsley
½–1 dl olive oil

► Slice the veal, put the slices in between sheets of plastic foil and beat them thin. Peel the onion and chop small. Shred the parsley. Mix the minced veal with the onion and parsley. Chop the anchovies and peeled garlic and stir them into the mince. Cut the cheese into sticks. Put out the slices of meat on the worktop. Put a small dob of mince and a stick of cheese on each one. Season with salt and black pepper. Drizzle with olive oil. Roll up each slice and secure with a toothpick.

Grill the veal olives all round on the grill or in the frying pan for about 10 minutes, until they are cooked all through. Arrange on a serving dish and garnish with slices of cheese, parsley and olive oil.

Air-dried venison sausage

15–20 servings

800 g venison (of roe deer)
125 g lard
20 g salt
5 g milled black pepper
7 g caster sugar
3 g nitrite salt
½ tbsp whole fennel seeds
1 metre natural (curved) casings

► Chop the venison and lard small and mix with the spices. Rinse the casings thoroughly and stuff with the farce; the easiest way of doing this is with an icing bag and a metal sausage stuffer. Take care to pack the sausage evenly. Hang it up in a place with a temperature of 5–8 °C and 70% air humidity. Leave it there for 5–7 days, depending on how firm you want it. If the atmosphere is too warm or dry the sausage will dry too fast, in which case it will get so hard that it will not be properly cured in the middle.

Marinating game

15–20 servings

1 kg game
Marinade:
3 tbsp salt
3 tbsp caster sugar
1 tbsp black pepper, crushed fine
2 tbsp flat-leafed parsley, chopped small
½ tbsp basil leaves, chopped small
½ tbsp thyme leaves, chopped small

► Divide the meat in two. Mix all the marinade ingredients together and rub the mixture into the meat. Put the two pieces of meat into a plastic bag and then into a mixing bowl. Marinate for 2 days in the fridge. Remove the meat from the bag and rinse it quickly in cold water. Wipe it dry and put it in a mould lined with plastic foil. Store in the freezer. Serve thinly sliced.

Terrine of omelette à la paysanne

20 servings

10 boiled potatoes
2 red onions
200 g smoked side pork or boiled ham
200 g button mushrooms
6 tbsp butter
8 eggs
½ dl whipping cream
1 dl shredded parsley

▶ Set the oven to 125 °C. Peel and dice the potatoes, onion and pork. Clean, trim and slice the mushrooms. Fry the potatoes, onion, pork and mushrooms separately in half the butter. Beat the eggs and cream together. Stir in the parsley. Mix the potato, pork, mushroom and onion together in the frying pan. Add the remaining butter, a knob at a time, and pour on the egg mixture. Put the pan on the hob. When the mixture starts to solidify, transfer the frying pan to the oven. Bake the omelette in the oven for about 10 minutes. Turn it out onto a plate. Put another plate on top to weigh it down and leave it to cool for about 1 hour. Cut the omelette in strips and then slice.

"Small warms"

This round includes many well-known classics. In a lot of people's minds, the smörgåsbord is associated with meatballs and Jansson's Temptation, both of which make their appearance in this round. You will also find a number of other popular dishes such as spare ribs, dip in the pot, lutfisk, chipolatas and various forms of cabbage, not forgetting a good many local variants, such as Småland potato dumplings and "long cabbage" from Halland.

Jansson's Temptation has a history of its own – in fact, two histories of its own. According to one of them, the entertainer Per Adolf "Pelle" Janzon made a name for himself in the closing years of the 19th century by giving his guests snaps together with a Swedish anchovy au gratin which was purportedly a concoction of his own devising. Sweden's Gastronomic Academy apparently attributes the name to a cook preparing the dish for a dinner party in the Östermalm district of Stockholm and, with Madam's permission, naming it after a Swedish film of that title.

Enna's Meatballs as served at Den Gyldene Freden, Stockholm

10–20 servings
50–60 meatballs:
1 kg pork and beef mince
½ dl dried breadcrumbs
1 dl milk
1 tbsp onion powder
1 tbsp salt
2½ pinches of ground black pepper
50 g butter

► Mix the milk and breadcrumbs together, then leave them to swell for about 5 minutes before mixing with the mince and spices. Take care the mince doesn't get warm in the meantime. Put the mince in the fridge for 30 minutes, then shape it into meatballs and fry them golden all round in butter till they are done.

Venison stew

10–12 servings
1 kg venison, shoulder or loin
2 tbsp butter
2 dl red wine
¾ dl red wine vinegar
2 tbsp tomato purée
1 litre game stock, concentrated
3 cm fresh ginger, grated
salt
black pepper
2–3 tbsp cornflour starch
Bouquet garni:
2 cloves of garlic, peeled
2 star anises
1 bay leaf
1 caraway capsule
1 small red chilli, e.g. Spanish pepper
gauze
trussing string
Garnish:
ceps sautéed in butter
carrots sautéed in butter
chopped leek sautéed in butter

► Mix the ingredients for the bouquet garni in the gauze and tie up with the trussing string. Dice the meat and brown it all over in butter. Add the wine, vinegar and tomato purée. Let the liquid soak in. Pour on the concentrated stock and bring to the boil. Put in the bouquet garni. Cover and cook for 1–1½ hours. Remove the meat and bouquet garni. Strain the stock and thicken with the cornflour starch dissolved in a little cold water.

Mix the meat and sauce before serving. Garnish with the ceps and vegetables.

Spare ribs off the bone with 5 spices

4–6 servings or about 15 for a smörgåsbord
1 kg thick salt flitch of pork (ribs will do, but make sure they're salted)
2 l chicken stock
water if needed
1 bay leaf
8 white peppercorns
1 red chilli, deseeded
1 tbsp chopped ginger
2 star anises
1 stick of cinnamon
3 whole cloves
1 tbsp fennel seeds
1 orange, sliced
1 onion, peeled and divided
1 carrot, peeled and cut up
½ dl honey
½ dl golden syrup
½ dl Japanese soy

► Put the meat into a casserole. Pour on the chicken stock and, if needed, enough water to cover. Bring to the boil and skim well. Add the spices, orange, green vegetables, honey, syrup and soy. Cover and simmer for about 2 hours. Remove the meat and leave to cool. Strain off the liquid and reduce till syrupy.

Set the oven to 225 °C. Cut the meat into serving-size portions and turn them in the sauce. Grill them in the oven for 10–15 minutes, till they are crisp and golden on the outside.

Game meatballs

50–70 meat balls
1 dl day-old white bread,
grated
2 dl milk
2 tbsp grated onion
300 g elk mince
100 g minced pork
1 tsp salt
1 egg
1 pinch of "4 spices" (clove,
nutmeg, ginger, pepper)
3 dl whipping cream
For frying:
butter

► Mix the bread and milk and
leave to swell for 5 minutes.
Fry the onion in butter and
leave to cool. Mix the mince
and salt together. Add the
bread-and-milk mixture, onion,
egg and spices. Dilute with the
cream. Mix to a smooth batter.
Roll meatballs and fry them
all round in butter till they are
done.

Fresh chipolatas

10–12 servings

20–25 chipolatas
175 g outer filet of veal
180 g lean shoulder of pork
150 g lard
9 g salt
2 g nitrite salt
2 g caster sugar
3 pinches of white pepper
1½ pinches of ginger, ground
1½ pinches of grated nutmeg
1 dl cold beef stock
5 metres of lamb casing, rinsed
in cold water
butcher's string

► Day 1: Dice the veal, pork
and lard. Mix them with the
salt, sugar and spices. Marinate
in the fridge for 3–4 hours.
Remove the meat and put
it twice through the mincer,
using the finest disc and
cooling it in between. Transfer
to a food processor and run
to a smooth mixture together
with the stock. Fry a sample to
test the seasoning. Stuff the
mixture into the casing, tying
into small chipolatas with the
butcher's string.

Day 2: Heat water in a
saucepan to about 70 °C.
Put in the chipolatas and
simmer them gently for about
30 minutes until the inner
temperature is 63–65 °C.
Remove them from the water,
wipe them dry and leave them
to cool.
Fry the chipolatas in butter
before serving.

Christmas or pork sausage

4–6 servings or 15–20 for a smörgåsbord

2–4 sausages:
250 g minced loin of pork
250 g minced beef
250 g minced pork
250 g boiled potatoes, grated
1 tbsp salt
½ tsp milled white pepper
½ tsp milled allspice
¼ tsp ground cloves
½ tsp ground ginger
½ tbsp potato flour
about 1½ dl meat stock
5 dl milk
1½ metres curved sausage casing

Saline mixture:
½ dl coarse salt
¼ dl caster sugar
½ tsp saltpetre (optional)

► Mix the cold meat, potato and spices in a food processor. Dilute with stock and milk while the machine is running. Test-cook a small dob of mince to check the seasoning. Transfer the sausage mixture to an icing bag with a large smooth nozzle. Oil the nozzle and the casing will slip on more easily. Squirt the mixture evenly into the casing, taking care to avoid bubbles. If you do

get an air bubble forming, prick a small hole in the casing and squeeze out the air. Mix the salt, sugar and saltpetre (if any) together. Rub the sausage with this mixture and store in a cold place overnight.

Heat water to 76 °C in a large saucepan. Put in the sausages and leave them there for about 45 minutes, till their inner temperature is 67 °C.

Yuletide stew with root vegetables, sharp cabbage and spicy sausage

4–6 servings or 15–20 for a smörgåsbord

4 potatoes
2 carrots
1 parsnip
1 white onion
500 g sauerkraut
4 dl chicken stock
1 dl dry white wine
1 tsp caraway
2 bay leaves
150 g boiled brisket of beef
100 g smoked pork/bacon
300 g boiled Christmas sausage (see recipe p. 132)

▶ Peel the root vegetables and cut them up. Peel and shred the onion. Boil them together with the sauerkraut, stock, wine and spices for 10 minutes. Add the brisket and pork/bacon and simmer for another 30 minutes. With five minutes left to go, cut up the Christmas sausage and add it to the pot.

Mustard and horse radish go well with this one, which can also be served away from the Christmas table on a cold afternoon in December.

Spicy sausage

20–25 servings

4-6 sausages:
250 g minced pork
50 g fine-ground minced chicken
25 g lard, minced
1½ pinches nitrite
½ tsp salt
½ pinch ground cloves
1 pinch ground fennel seeds
½ pinch milled white pepper
1 small shallot
½ dl water
½ dl Christmas ale
1 metre pork casing, rinsed clean

▶ Run he minced pork, minced chicken, lard, nitrite, salt and spices together for 1–2 minutes in the food processor. Leave for about 2 hours in the fridge. Peel the shallot and chop small. Boil it in a little water for 2–3 minutes. Leave to cool.

Stir water and ale into the mince. Work in the onion. Stuff the mixture into the casing.

Bring water and salt to the boil in a saucepan. Simmer the sausages for 12–15 minutes, to an inner temperature of 67 °C.

Jansson's Temptation
about 10 servings
10 medium-sized potatoes, about 1 kg
1 large onion
1 tin of "Swedish anchovy" filets (125 g)
1 dl milk
4 dl whipping cream
salt
white pepper

► Peel and shred the potato and onion. Chop the "anchovy" coarsely. Mix the potato, onion, "anchovy", "anchovy" liquor, milk and 3 dl whipping cream in a saucepan. Simmer on a low flame until the potato is nearly soft. Add a little more milk if necessary. Stir gently from time to time, to keep the potato from sticking. Season to taste. Transfer the mixture to an oven-proof dish. Leave to cool and put in the fridge for the night.

Set the oven to 225 °C. Pour on 1 dl whipping cream. Bake in the middle of the oven till golden brown.

Mushroom omelette
about 10 servings
6 eggs
1 dl whipping cream
1 tsp salt
1 pinch of milled white pepper
1 tbsp butter
Mushroom filling:
100 g mushrooms as available, e.g. chanterelles, ceps or button mushrooms
4 tbsp butter
½ dl white flour
4 dl milk
2 dl whipping cream
salt
milled white pepper
Garnish:
shredded flat-leafed parsley

► Start with the mushroom filling. Clean the mushrooms and cut them up. Sauté in butter. Sprinkle with the flour and sauté for another minute or so. Add the milk and stir till the flour dissolves. Pour on the whipping cream and boil the sauce, stirring continuously, for about 5 minutes. Season with salt and white pepper.

Beat the egg, whipping cream, salt and pepper together with a fork. Heat a frying pan with butter. Pour the egg mixture into the warm pan, after the butter has turned slightly golden. Stir carefully with a wooden spoon, to fry the omelette evenly. The omelette must solidify, but fluffily.

Pour the filling onto the omelette and garnish with shredded flat-leafed parsley.

Småland potato dumplings with pork
4–6 servings or 10–12 for a smörgåsbord
20–25 small "body cake" dumplings:
300 g salt pork
1 onion
about 1 tbsp crushed allspice
600 g cold boiled potato
100 g white flour
1 egg yolk

► Dice the pork small and crisp-fry it. Peel and chop the onion and fry till soft. Mix the pork, onion and allspice together.

Grate the potato with a fine grating disc and mix with the flour and egg yolk to make a dough. Shape into little balls. Make a depression in each one with your thumb, inserting 1 tsp of the pork mixture. Press the pork down while at the same time covering it over with the edges of the potato ball. Roll smooth and place on a lightly floured tea towel.

Bring lightly salted water to the boil in a large pot. Put the dumplings in one by one. Simmer gently till they float to the surface, then simmer for 5 minutes more.

Remove the dumplings with a slotted spoon and chill them immediately in iced water. Remove and drain on a tea towel. Store in the fridge and fry them in butter before serving.

Stewed Savoy cabbage

6 servings or 12 for a smörgås-bord

½ Savoy cabbage
½ shallot
1 tbsp butter
3 tbsp whipping cream
3 tbsp crème fraîche
3 tbsp chicken stock
1–2 pinches of salt

► Rinse and shred the cabbage. Boil lightly salted water in a saucepan. Put in the Savoy cabbage and boil for 3–4 minutes. Remove and cool in iced water. Drain well. Peel and chop the shallot. Sauté in butter till soft, without letting it change colour. Add the Savoy cabbage and pour on the cream, crème fraîche and chicken stock. Bring to the boil and simmer for 5 minutes. Add salt to taste.

Red cabbage

about 20 servings

1 kg red cabbage
3 sharp apples
3 tbsp butter
4 dl red wine
½ dl red wine vinegar
½ dl black currant juice
1 stick of cinnamon
1 bay leaf
2 star anises
4–6 whole cloves
1 tsp salt
white pepper

► Shred the cabbage in a food processor or with a sharp knife. Peel and dice the apples. Melt the butter in a large casserole and put in the cabbage. Add the apple, wine, vinegar, juice, spices and salt. Cover and cook over a low flame for 1½ hours, stirring regularly to keep from burning. Season with salt and white pepper.

Brown cabbage

about 20 servings

1 kg (white) cabbage
3 tbsp butter
2 dl dry white wine
½ dl white wine vinegar
1 dl golden syrup
1 stick of cinnamon
1 bay leaf
1 star anise
3 cloves, whole or crushed
salt
white pepper

► Shred the cabbage in a food processor or with a sharp knife. Melt the butter in a large pot, adding the cabbage and onion. Add the wine, vinegar, syrup, spices and salt. Cover and cook over a low flame for 1½ hours, stirring regularly to keep from burning. Season with salt and white pepper.

Curly kale

10–12 servings

500 g curly kale
1 shallot
1 tbsp butter
1 bay leaf
2 dl ham stock
5 dl whipping cream
salt
black pepper
50 g Christmas ham, diced

► Clean the kale and cut away the stalk. Bring lightly salted water to the boil. Dip the kale in the water for 1 minute. Peel and chop the shallot. Sauté in the butter. Add the kale, bay leaf, ham stock and cream. Boil till half the liquid remains. Season with salt and pepper. Mix in the diced ham and serve.

Wort bread

5 loaves

Day 1:
125 g coarse-ground rye flour
250 g small beer
Day 2:
200 g yeast
450 g small beer
250 g coarse-ground rye flour
1 kg white flour
375 g liquid wort
150 g black treacle
50 g butter
30 g wort spice
30 g salt
200 g raisins, soaked
milk for brushing

► Day 1: Put the rye flour into a mixing bowl. Bring the small beer to the boil and pour it over the rye flour. Mix together and cover with plastic foil. Leave at room temperature till the following day.

Day 2: Mix the yeast, small beer and rye flour together in a food processor or dough mixer for about 5 minutes. Cover with plastic foil and leave to rise for 30 or 40 minutes. Add the dough from day 1 and the rest of the ingredients. Run the dough for 8 or 10 minutes in a food processor until it has formed enough gluten and is

supple. Leave to stand for ½ hour.

Divide into 5 pieces and shape them into loaves, placing them in greased one-litre loaf tins or on baking trays lined with baking tray paper. Cover with plastic foil and leave to rise, without the plastic touching the bread or else under a moist tea towel, for 1–1½ hours in room temperature.

Set the oven to 250 °C. Put the loaves in when the oven is warm and lower the temperature immediately to 200 °C. It is a good idea to spray a little

water in the oven with a spray bottle, to generate steam.

Bake the loaves for 20 or 25 minutes, until the inner temperature is 98 °C. Remove them from the oven, tip them out if you have been using loaf tins, and place them on a wire rack. Brush the tops with milk for a soft and shiny surface. Leave them to cool, then put them into plastic bags.

Dip in the pot

Use the stock left over from boiling the ham or the pig's trotters.

Brisket of beef in summer vegetables

10–12 servings
1 kg salted brisket
1 dl dry white wine
1 bay leaf
2 sprigs of thyme
6 whole black peppercorns
2 sprigs of parsley
Vegetables:
3 young carrots
10 spring onions
10-15 small potatoes
1 dl plucked parsley leaves
1 pinch of salt
1 pinch of caster sugar
1 tsp white wine vinegar

► Rinse the brisket in cold water for 10 minutes. Put it in a saucepan. Pour on enough wine and water to cover. Bring to the boil. Skim carefully. Add the bay leaf, thyme, black pepper and sprigs of parsley. Cover and simmer for about 2 hours.

Add the carrots, spring onions and potatoes. Simmer for another 20 minutes. Remove the brisket and vegetables. Dice them. Return them to the stock together with the parsley leaves. Add salt, sugar and vinegar to taste.

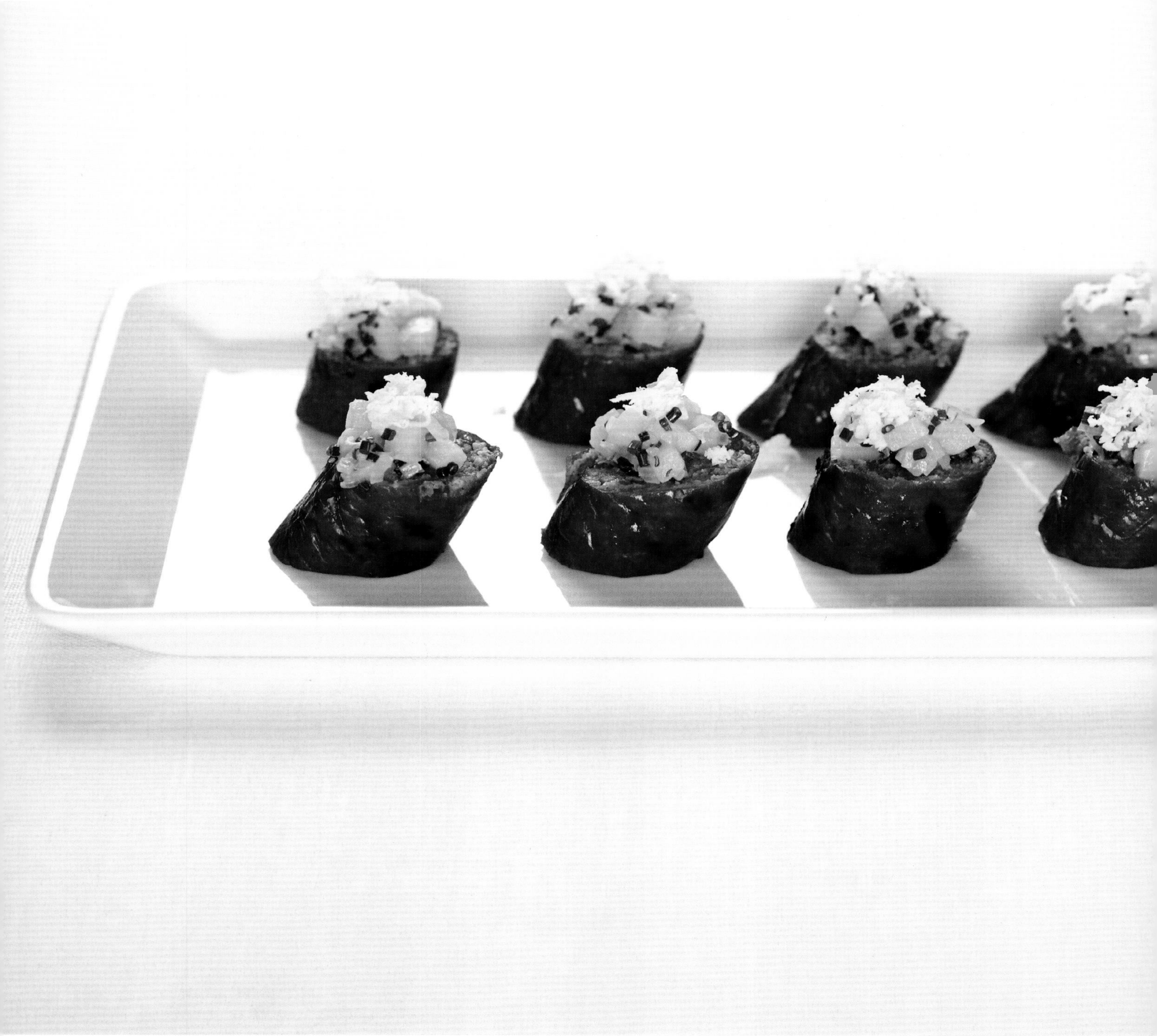

Isterband sausage with apple salad

10–12 servings
2 *Isterband* sausages
1 green apple
½ dl grated horseradish
1 tbsp shredded chives
1 tsp olive oil
► Fry the *Isterband* sausage gently in a frying pan, making sure it doesn't split. Leave to cool. Cut slices about 1 cm thick and arrange them on a dish with the cut surface uppermost. Peel the apple and dice small. Mix with the horseradish, chives and oil. Top each piece of *Isterband* with a little apple salad.

Grilled chicken

6 servings or 12 for a smörgås-bord

1 chicken, weighing about
1½ kg
9½ dl water
60 g salt
1 pinch of salt
½ pinch of black pepper
1 tsp plucked thyme leaves
2 tbsp olive oil
1 tbsp liquid honey

► Day 1: Wipe the chicken with kitchen tissue. Bring salt water to the boil, then leave to cool. Put the chicken in and store in the fridge overnight.

Day 2: Set the oven to 175 °C. Remove the chicken and wipe it with kitchen tissue. Truss it with the legs and wings close to the body. Mix the salt, pepper, thyme and olive oil together in a bowl. Brush the chicken with the oil. Roast it in the oven for about 45 minutes. Remove and baste with honey. Raise the oven temperature to 200 °C and roast for another 5–7 minutes, till the chicken is golden. Carve and serve on a dish. To make the skin extra crisp, you can remove it and roast it longer in the oven or deep-fry it in oil.

Pike-perch baked in foil

10–12 servings

400–500 g pike-perch
9 ½ dl water
50 g salt
1 red onion
1 bunch of dill
2 tbsp butter
40 whole black peppercorns, crushed
1 tsp whole allspice corns, crushed
2 tbsp olive oil
2 tbsp dry white wine

► Bring the water and salt to the boil. Trim the pike-perch filet and cut it into small serving portions. Immerse these in the brine for about 2 hours. Peel the red onion and cut it into strips. Rough-chop the dill.

Set the oven to 150 °C. Remove the pike-perch from the brine and wipe it dry with kitchen tissue. Put two large sheets of aluminium foil, each about 50 cm, on top of each other on the worktop. Grease the foil in the middle with a little of the butter.

Place the pieces of pike-perch on the greased foil. Put the onion, dill, spices and remaining knobs of butter on top of them. Drizzle with olive oil and wine. Fold the sheets of foil together to make a bag, closing all openings. Bake on the middle shelf of the oven for about 15 minutes (alternatively, put the foil parcel on the grill for 10 or 15 minutes).

Veal in dill sauce

10–12 servings

1 kg shoulder of veal, off the bone
1 leek
2 carrots
10 white peppercorns
2 tsp salt
3 dill stalks
1 bay leaf
Sauce:
1 tbsp butter

2 tbsp white flour
5 dl stock from boiling the meat
1½ tbsp distilled vinegar (12%, *ättika*)
1–2 tbsp caster sugar
salt (optional)
2 tbsp chopped dill
2 tbsp chopped fresh spinach
1 egg yolk

► Dice the veal. Trim the leek and cut it in pieces. Peel and

cut up the carrots. Bring water to the boil in a casserole. Put in the meat and simmer for 5 minutes. Drain off the water. Pour on fresh water, enough to cover the meat. Bring to the boil and skim. Add the spices and vegetables. Simmer the meat for about 2 hours. Remove the meat, strain the stock and save 5 dl for the sauce.

Melt the butter in a saucepan and stir in the flour. Sauté for 2 minutes. Pour on the stock and boil for about 5 minutes, stirring continuously. Add *ättika* and sugar to taste, and perhaps salt as well. Mix the sauce with the dill, spinach and egg yolk. Fold in the veal and serve immediately.

Lutfisk with white sauce

4–6 servings or 10–12 for a smörgåsbord
1 kg *lutfisk* (stockfish)
1 tsp salt
White sauce:
2 tbsp butter
3 tbsp white flour
4 dl milk
2 dl whipping cream
grated nutmeg
salt
white pepper
Garnish:
50 g crisp-fried pork

► Day 1. Rinse the *lutfisk* (stockfish) in running cold water till the water runs clear. Leave it in water overnight.

Day 2. Set the oven to 200 °C. Put the fish into an oven-proof dish and cover with aluminium foil. Cook in the middle of the oven for about 30 minutes. Remove the *lutfisk* and let it rest before serving.

Melt the butter in a saucepan. Stir in the flour and sauté, stirring continuously, for about 3 minutes. Add warm milk, stirring continuously. Pour in the cream. Cook for another 5 minutes, stirring all the time. Add nutmeg, salt and pepper to taste. Serve the *lutfisk* with the sauce, clarified butter, crisp-fried side pork and purée of green peas.

Purée of green peas

4 servings
1 shallot, chopped small
1 tbsp butter
2 dl green peas
1 dl crème fraîche
salt and pepper

► Sauté the onion in butter in a saucepan. Pour in the peas and crème fraîche. Simmer for about 3 minutes. Run the mixture to a purée in the food processor. Season with salt and pepper. Serve with the *lutfisk*.

Brown beans

15 servings
4 dl dried brown beans
about 6 dl chicken stock
water
salt
2 tbsp distilled vinegar
(*ättika*, 12% strength)
2–3 tbsp golden syrup
1 tbsp salt
pepper to taste
► Put the beans to soak in
water and salt, 1tbsp salt per
liter of water, for at least 12
hours in room temperature.
Drain, and rinse in cold
water. Mix with the chicken
stock. Boil the beans for
about 1 hour, till soft. If they
are too soggy you can firm
them up with a little potato
flour, and if they are too thick
you can dilute with a little
water. Add distilled vinegar
and syrup to taste, and perhaps salt and pepper too.

The green round

Today it seems only natural that vegetarian dishes should have a round of their own on the smörgåsbord. Apart from many people being vegetarians, most other guests appreciate a good selection of vegetables and vegetable compositions. The green round imparts a breath of fresh air to the smörgåsbord, and opportunity of decking it with fresh spring vegetables or the root vegetables and legumes of autumn.

Warm cep salad
10–12 servings
600–800 g assorted mush-
rooms, e.g. ceps, shiitake,
button mushrooms and chanterelles
3 tbsp butter
1 shallot
1 tbsp shredded parsley
1 tbsp olive oil
1 dl lettuce shoots and herbs
► Trim the mushrooms. Fry
them in butter, adding salt
and pepper to taste. Drain on
kitchen tissue. Peel the onion
and chop small. Mix the onion,
parsley and olive oil. Mix the
mushrooms together with the
herb oil and lettuce shoots in
a mixing bowl. Put the mushrooms on a serving dish and
drizzle with a little of the oil.

Foil-wrapped onions

10 servings

2 tbsp butter
1 kg tender spring onions, yellow and red
3 tbsp olive oil
10 sprigs of lemon thyme
1 tsp sea salt

► Set the oven to 150 °C or light the grill. Spread a sheet of aluminium foil, 50 x 50 cm, folded double, on a worktop and grease it with a little of the butter. Rinse the onion and cut off the haulm. Make a cm deep incision in each onion. Now place the onions on the foil and dab them with the remaining butter. Pour the olive oil over this and sprinkle with thyme sprigs and sea salt. Now fold the foil into a package, making sure it is leak-proof. Roast the package in the oven for about 30 minutes or put it on the grill and bake it close to the embers for about 30 minutes. (Don't let the embers get too hot.) Remove from the heat and leave to stand for about 5 minutes. Slit open the foil and serve, but watch out for the hot steam escaping from the package.

Potato salad with hazelnut oil

8–10 servings

500 g fresh-cooked, warm potatoes
2 tbsp plucked curly parsley
2 tbsp plucked dill
2 tbsp shredded spring onion
1 small red onion, chopped

Vinaigrette:
1 tbsp chopped shallot
3 tbsp sherry vinegar
1 tsp Dijon mustard
2 tbsp hazelnut oil
2 tbsp grape seed oil
½ tsp sea salt
1 pinch of black pepper

► Mix all the vinaigrette ingredients together in a lidded glass jar. Shake vigorously. Cut up the potatoes. Mix them with the vinaigrette and leave to stand for about 1 hour. Dredge in the parsley, dill, spring onion and red onion.

Red cabbage with caraway and orange

8–10 servings

½ red cabbage
1 tbsp salt
1 tbsp caster sugar
½ red onion
1 dl mayonnaise
1 dl crème fraîche
1 tbsp apple cider vinegar
1 tsp caraway
1 orange, grated zest of
1 tsp salt
1 pinch of black pepper

► Shred the red cabbage into narrow strips and sprinkle with salt and sugar. Cover with plastic foil and leave to stand at room temperature for 2 hours. Peel and shred the onion. Squeeze the moisture out of the cabbage and mix the cabbage with onion, mayonnaise, crème fraîche, vinegar, caraway and orange zest. Season with salt and black pepper.

Cabbage salad with apple

8–10 servings

½ small cabbage
2 sharp green apples
1 tsp pressed lemon juice
3 tbsp crème fraîche
2 tsp stewed apple
about 1 tbsp calvados
½ tsp salt

► Shred the cabbage and dip it briefly in lightly salted water. Leave to drain. De-core the apple and cut it into narrow strips. Mix these with the lemon juice, crème fraîche, stewed apple and calvados. Stir in the cabbage. Season with salt.

Asian red cabbage salad

8–10 servings

½ red cabbage
1 jalapeño chilli
½ dl rice vinegar
3 tbsp Thai fish sauce
2 tbsp caster sugar
a dash of Tabasco

► Shred the cabbage fine. Deseed the chilli and chop small. Mix the cabbage in a mixing bowl with the chili, rice vinegar, fish sauce and sugar. Add a dash or so of Tabasco to taste and stir. Cover with plastic foil and store in the fridge for 2 days to marinate it and bring out the flavours.

Carrot terrine

12 servings
500 g baby carrots
4 dl carrot juice
2 dl pressed orange juice
15 g fresh ginger, grated
2 sheets of gelatine
7 g agar agar

► Peel the carrots. Bring the carrot juice, orange juice and ginger to the boil. Cook the carrots in the juice till they are soft. Soak the sheets of gelatine in cold water for about 5 minutes. Strain the reduced carrot stock and beat in the agar agar. Bring to the boil and simmer for 1 minute. Remove from the heat and leave to cool. Remove the sheets of gela-

tine from the water and melt them in the stock.

Pack the carrots into a plastic-lined terrine mould, 3 x 15 cm. Pour reduced stock in between, making sure that no air bubbles are allowed to form. Cover the mould with plastic foil and place on a chopping board. Store in a cold place for at least 12 hours with a weight on top. Cut through the plas-

tic with a warm knife when serving.

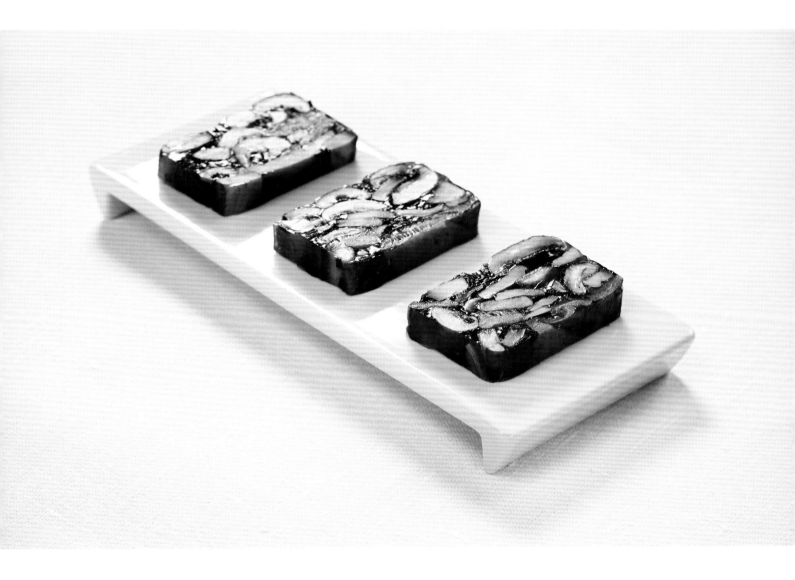

Mushroom brawn

15 servings

1 kg mushrooms, e.g. shiitake, button mushrooms, oys-
ter mushrooms, porcini and
chanterelles
2 tbsp butter
8 sheets of gelatine
2 tbsp parsley, shredded fine
and blanched
salt
black pepper
1 tbsp white balsamic
vinegar

Stock:
½ kg assorted mushrooms
1 onion
2 tbsp butter
1 dl dry white wine
7½ dl water
► Begin with the stock. Trim
and chop the mushrooms.
Peel and chop the onion.
Sauté the onion in half the
butter. Add the wine and
cook till all the liquid has
been absorbed. Add the
remaining butter, put in the

mushrooms and fry for about
5 minutes. Pour on the water
and simmer for about 20
minutes, skimming well all
the time. Strain the stock.

Clean and trim the mush-
rooms and cut them into dif-
ferently sized pieces – the
small ones can be left as they
are. Sauté the mushrooms in
butter. Soak the sheets of
gelatine in cold water for
about 5 minutes. Heat the
stock. Remove the sheets of

gelatine from the water and
melt them in the stock. Stir in
the parsley and add salt,
pepper and vinegar to taste.

Fill a plastic-lined terrine
mould, 4 x 20 cm, with the
mushroom mixture. Pour on
the stock, a little at a time,
making sure it penetrates
everywhere and that no air
pockets are formed. Refrigerate for at least 12 hours with
a weight on top.

Summer salad

4 servings

1 dl plucked frisée lettuce, the innermost leaves
1 dl plucked small romaine lettuce leaves
2 dl mixed lettuce shots and herbs
1 dl plucked leaves of various flowers, e.g. violet and pansy
2 tbsp olive oil

► Pluck all the leaves and, for a crispy salad, soak them for 20 minutes in iced water. Pour off the water and dry the lettuce in a lettuce drier. Arrange the salad on a serving dish and drizzle with olive oil.

Poached cauliflower

10 servings

500 g cauliflower
½ tsp salt
½ dl distilled vinegar (*ättika*, 12% strength)
1 dl caster sugar
1½ dl water
1 tsp yellow mustard seeds
2 bay leaves
1 shallot, sliced
½ dl plucked crown dill

► Break up the cauliflower into small florets. Bring salted water to the boil and simmer the cauliflower until it begins to soften but remains a little crispy. Remove and chill in iced water. Bring distilled vinegar, sugar, water, mustard seeds, bay leaves and shallot to the boil. Remove from the heat and leave to cool. Add the cauliflower and crown dill when the pickling liquid is cold. Refrigerate overnight, for the cauliflower to absorb the flavour.

Crispy beans

10 servings

3 dl sugar snap peas or beans
½ tsp salt
1 tbsp chopped shallot
1 tbsp olive oil
½ tbsp shredded mint

1–2 tsp sea salt

► Top and tail the beans. Bring lightly salted water to the boil. Simmer the beans quickly, for 30–60 seconds. Chill in ice water, to keep them crisp. Remove the beans and wipe them dry with a tea towel. Mix them with the shallot, olive oil, mint and sea salt.

Pickled root vegetables and trumpet chanterelles

8–10 servings
2 parsnips
2 carrots
2 yellow carrots
200 g celeriac
200 g trumpet chanterelles
4 dl 1–2–3 pickling liquid (see herring recipe)
1 bay leaf
6 white peppercorns
1 clove
1 small stick of cinnamon
½ dl plucked dill
1 tbsp cold-pressed rape-seed oil

► Peel the root vegetables and cut them up. Boil them in lightly salted water till soft. Remove and drain on a tea towel. Bring lightly salted water to the boil and dip the trumpet chanterelles in it for about 30 seconds. Put them to drain on a tea towel. Mix the pickling liquid with the spices, chanterelles and root vegetables. Store in the fridge for at least 2 days. Strain the root vegetables and chanterelles before serving. Dredge them in dill and rapeseed oil.

Citrus-marinated fennel

10 servings
2 fennels
1 tbsp honey
½ lemon, grated zest of
½ dl pressed lemon
2 tbsp olive oil
1 pinch sea salt

► Cut the fennel into thin strips and soak these in iced water for about 20 minutes, reserving the dill-like sprigs for garnish. Mix together the honey, lemon zest and juice and olive oil. Mix the fennel, the marinade and the fennel dill together just before serving.

A cup of raw vegetables

10 servings
2 carrots
½ cucumber
½ bunch of celery
1 small romaine lettuce
Balsamic vinaigrette:
1 clove of garlic
½ dl balsamic vinegar
2 tsp honey
1 dl grape seed oil
½ tsp sea salt
1 pinch of fresh-milled black pepper

► Peel the carrots and cucumber and cut them into sticks. Divide the celery stalks in two and cut them into sticks. Pluck the lettuce leaves. Put all the vegetables into cups. Mix all the vinaigrette ingredients together in a lidded jar, shaking to mix thoroughly. Transfer to a bowl and serve with the vegetables.

Pickled cucumber

10 servings
500 g cucumber
½ dl distilled vinegar (*ättika*, 12% strength)
1 dl caster sugar
1½ dl water
1 pinch brown mustard seeds
1 bay leaf
2 tbsp plucked crown dill

► Peel and de-core the cucumber. Cut it into small cubes. Bring the *ättika*, sugar, water, mustard sees and bay leaf to the boil. Leave to cool. Mix the cucumber and crown dill into the liquid. Refrigerate overnight.

Fresh-picked lettuce
10 servings
5 dl assorted lettuce leaves, e.g. crisp, lollo rosso, purslane, mâché, romaine
2 tbsp plucked curly parsley
1 tbsp chopped shallot
1 tbsp plucked chervil
1 dl plucked red mangold leaves or young beetroot leaves
Classic vinaigrette:
2 tbsp chopped shallot
3½ tbsp sherry vinegar
4 tbsp grape seed oil
1 pinch of sea salt
1 pinch of fresh-milled black pepper

► Pluck all the lettuce leaves and herbs in small sprigs. Put both lettuce and herbs to soak in iced water for 20 minutes, to make the lettuce crispy. Pour off the water and dry the lettuce in a lettuce drier. Mix the vinaigrette and serve with the salad.

Salad of common beans and runner beans

(for a vegetarian version, skip the bacon)

10 servings

250 g common beans
250 g runner beans
½ tsp salt
250 g bacon

1 small red onion
2 tbsp shredded parsley
2 tbsp cold-pressed rapeseed oil
½ tsp sea salt
1 pinch of fresh-milled black pepper

► Top and tail the beans and bring lightly salted water to the boil. Simmer the beans for about 2 minutes, leaving them with a crispy core. Remove and chill in iced water. Cut the bacon into cubes and crisp-fry them. Leave to drain on kitchen tissue. Peel the red onion and cut it into strips. Arrange the beans on a serving dish and sprinkle the bacon, onion, parsley and rapeseed oil over them. Season with sea salt and black pepper.

Boiled, pickled beetroot
10 servings
1 kg mixed beetroot – small ones, yellow ones, and lyophilised table beet
1 dl distilled vinegar (*ättika*, 12% strength)
2 dl caster sugar
3 dl water
2 tbsp olive oil
2 dl plucked tender beetroot leaves or mangold shoots
► Trim all the beetroot and boil them separately in water without peeling them first. Remove and peel under the cold tap. Bring *ättika*, sugar and water to the boil. Leave to cool. Mix the beetroot together in the pickling liquid and refrigerate overnight.

Remove the beetroot and drain them on kitchen tissue. Cut them into slices or wedges or leave them whole. Arrange them on a serving dish. Drizzle with olive oil and sprinkle with tender leaves and a little flake salt.

Coloured carrots

10 servings

600 g tender baby carrots of various colours – yellow, orange, red, mauve

½ tbsp caster sugar

1 tbsp butter

1 tbsp olive oil

3 tbsp plucked curly parsley

1 tsp sea salt

► Set the oven to 125 °C. Peel and trim the carrots. Put them into an oven-proof dish, sprinkle them with sugar and knobs of butter and drizzle with olive oil. Stir a little. Cover with aluminium foil and roast in the middle of the oven for 25–30 minutes.

Leave to cool, then serve with the curly parsley, sea salt and the liquid remaining in the dish.

Leek and egg salad

10 servings

2 tender young leeks
½ tsp salt
4 hard-boiled eggs
3 tbsp capers
1–2 tbsp cold-pressed rapeseed oil
½ tsp sea salt

▶ Trim the leek and cut it into lengths of about 5 cm. Remove the outermost leaves and rinse under the cold tap. Bring lightly salted water to the boil and simmer the leeks until they are soft. Remove and chill in iced water. Shell and chop the eggs. Chop the capers. Serve the leek with eggs, capers and rapeseed oil. Sprinkle with sea salt.

Spelt salad with lemon vinaigrette

10 servings
2 dl pearl spelt or pearl barley, hulled
½ tsp salt
2 dl small red tomatoes
10 plucked basil leaves
3 dl lettuce leaves, e.g. purslane, crisp lettuce, mangold shoots
1 tbsp shredded parsley
Lemon vinaigrette:
1¼ dl pressed lemon
1¼ dl olive oil
½ tsp sea salt
1 pinch of fresh-milled black pepper

► Bring lightly salted water to the boil and boil the spelt grains in it till they are soft. Drain the spelt and rinse it under the cold tap to cool it and keep it from turning into a sticky mass. Drain. Mix the spelt grains with halved tomatoes, basil, lettuce and parsley.

Mix the lemon juice, olive oil, salt and pepper in a screw-top jar. Shake to mix the vinaigrette thoroughly and then pour it over the salad.

Grilled green asparagus

10 servings
500 g green asparagus
1 tbsp olive oil
1 tbsp sea salt
1 tsp grated lemon zest
1 pinch of fresh-milled black
pepper

► Trim the asparagus, peeling
it if necessary. Rub it with olive
oil and grill for 3–4 minutes in
the grill, leaving it a little al
dente. Arrange on a dish. Mix
the sea salt and lemon zest
together. Sprinkle the asparagus with this and the pepper.

Multicoloured tomatoes
10 servings
600 g assorted small tomatoes – red, yellow, orange and dark green
2 tbsp tender basil leaves
1 tbsp olive oil
½ tsp sea salt
1 pinch of fresh-milled black pepper

► Rinse the tomatoes and cut them up, halving some, slicing others or cutting them in wedges, and leaving one or two whole. Arrange them on a serving dish. Put the basil leaves on top. Pour olive oil over them and sprinkle with salt and pepper.

Tomato salad with sorrel

10 servings

600 g assorted small tomatoes – red, yellow and dark green
1 little red onion
1 dl pearl spelt or barley, boiled
2 dl plucked sorrel
Lemon vinaigrette:

1¼ dl pressed lemon
1¼ dl olive oil
1 tbsp honey
½ tsp sea salt
1 pinch of fresh-milled black pepper

► Rinse and halve the tomatoes. Peel and chop the red onion. Mix the tomatoes, red onion, pearl spelt/barley and sorrel together. Mix the lemon juice, olive oil, honey, salt and pepper together in a screw-top jar, shaking it to mix thoroughly. Serve the vinaigrette with the tomato salad.

Cheese

Sweden is the promised land of cheeses, and the average Swede gets through 18.5 kilos a year. Spiced hard cheese goes perfectly with the herring in the first round, and SOS (meaning butter-cheese-herring) is a big Swedish standby. Spiced cheese is a Swedish phenomenon and caraway cheese is simply delicious together with caraway-flavoured aquavit. Serving cheese with fish is standard Swedish smörgåsbord practice and probably unknown in any other culinary tradition. Some people prefer to skip the cheese, but on the modern smörgåsbord, in our opinion, it deserves a round to itself.

The monks, who first came to Sweden in the 11th century, were skilled cheesewrights and their know-how laid the foundations of a long tradition of hard cheeses. Hard cheese today is just about as Swedish as it gets. Many of the cheeses are still known by their old monastic names – Wästgöta Kloster ("Västergötland Monastery"), for example. Herrgård ("Manor House"), Grevé ("The Count"), Präst ("Parson's Cheese") and Svecia, those classic Swedish favourites, are an inalienable part of our heritage.

Cheeses, from top: Wästgöta Kloster (Monastery, Krydd (Spiced), Cheddar, herrgård (Manor House), svecia, prästost (Parson's).

Cheese terrine
10–12 servings
250 g mature *prästost*, grated
2 tbsp crème fraîche
1 cl Norrlands Akvavit (snaps)
½ pinch of cayenne pepper
100 g *wästgöta kloster-krydd*, diced
75 g *herrgård*, diced
75 g *svecia*, diced

► Put the *prästost* cheese in a saucepan with the crème fraîche. Melt gently over a low flame. Season with the snaps and cayenne pepper. Fold the cheese cubes into the mixture and stir. Transfer the whole mixture to a mould, 20 x 4 cm, lined with plastic foil and put it in the fridge to set. Serve sliced.

Akvavit raisins
10–12 servings
100 g large yellow raisins
3 cl Akvavit (snaps) – any kind
► Mix the raisins and snaps together in a plastic bag. Squeeze out the air and tie up. Refrigerate for at least 3 days, while the raisins marinate. Serve with cheese.

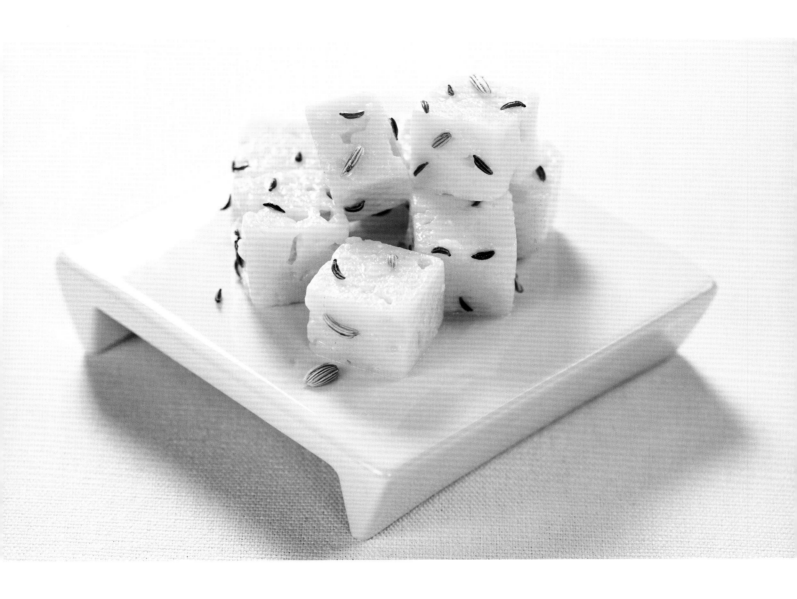

Svecia cheese flavoured with O.P. Anderson snaps

10-12 servings

300 g well-ripened *svecia* cheese
1 tsp roasted fennel seeds
1 tsp roasted caraway seeds
4 cl O.P. Anderson snaps
2 tsp rapeseed oil

► Cut the cheese into cubes. Transfer to a jar and add the spices, the O.P. Anderson snaps and the oil. Shake gently and refrigerate for at least 2 days, for the cheese to absorb the flavour. Serve with herring.

Potted cheese

6-10 servings

1 dl milk
4 cl spiced snaps or beer
200 g assorted cheese
1 tsp aniseed, coarse-crushed
1 tsp caraway, coarse-crushed
1 pinch of black pepper
1–2 pinches salt

► Heat the milk and snaps/beer. Pour into a food proces-sor and add the cheese. Run to a smooth mixture, adding more liquid if needed. Add the spices to taste. Transfer the mixture to a jar and store in the fridge until served.

Desserts

After all these salt, smoked and pickled delights, the time has come to restore the body's equilibrium with something sweet. We have dwelt a good deal on childhood memories like berries on straw, cheese cake, Maltese rice and strawberries, but we have also included beautiful lingonberry pears, a divine chocolate pie and a refreshing passion fruit pudding.

**Stewed pears with a lingon-
berry, black currant or
saffron flavour**
For black currant or saffron
pears, replace the lingonberries with black currants or two
5g sachets of saffron.
15–20 servings
1½ kg lingonberry
1–1½ litres water
2 kg Swedish pears
600 g caster sugar/litre juice
1 cinnamon stick
2 star anises
peel of 2 Seville oranges
► Cook the lingonberries in
water till they disintegrate.
Strain through a cheese cloth.
Measure out sugar for the
lingonberry juice. Bring the
juice to the boil and skim it.
Peel the pears, cutting a cross
in the bottom of each one
to help the juice penetrate.
Add the cinnamon, star anise,
Seville orange peel and peeled
pears to the lingonberry juice.
Remove the star anises after
5 minutes. Cook the pears till
they are soft. Remove them
and reduce the liquid by half.
Put the pears in a glass jar and
pour the liquid over them.

Leave to cool, then store in
the fridge for a few days to
mature.

Lingonberry and vanilla pudding

10–12 servings or 20 for a smörgåsbord

Vanilla yoghurt pudding:
2 sheets of gelatine
½ vanilla pod
3 tbsp caster sugar
3 dl whipping cream
2 dl yoghurt naturel, 10%
White chocolate mousse:
200 g white chocolate
5 dl whipping cream
Lingonberries:
1½ dl lingonberries
4 tbsp caster sugar
1 tsp liquid honey
Garnish:
crumbled ginger snaps
white chocolate, grate

► Mix the lingonberries with the sugar and honey.

Soak the sheets of gelatine in cold water for about 5 minutes. Split the vanilla pod and scrape out the seeds. Bring the sugar and cream to the boil together with the vanilla pod and seeds. Leave aside for 10 minutes. Transfer the gelatine sheets to the cream mixture to melt. Fold in the yoghurt and strain. Put out in glasses and refrigerate to set.

Chop the chocolate and put it in a saucepan together with the cream. Melt over a low flame. Mix with a stick blender. Refrigerate overnight or for at least 6 hours. Whisk the mousse slowly to the right consistency. If you whisk it too fast it may curdle. Cover the pudding with the lingonberries and spread white chocolate mousse on top. Crumble gingersnap and white chocolate over it.

Sea buckthorn chocolate
10–12 servings or 20 for a smörgåsbord
Chocolate cream:
90 g dark chocolate
125 g whipping cream
125 g milk
3 egg yolks
50 g caster sugar
1 sheet of gelatine
Toffee cream:
1 tin of condensed milk (397 g)
Sea buckthorn mousse:
2 sheets of gelatine
200 g sea buckthorn purée
1 orange, pressed juice of
3 tbsp caster sugar
2 dl whipping cream, lightly whipped
Garnish:
brownie croutons
chocolate sticks

► Chop the chocolate. Bring the cream and milk to the boil. Mix the egg yolks and sugar together. Soak the sheet of gelatine in cold water for about 5 minutes. Pour the warm cream over the egg yolks and stir. Heat gently, stirring all the time, to 82 °C. Pour the warm mixture over the chocolate and stir to a smooth mixture. Remove the gelatine from the water and melt it in the chocolate. Stir smooth and transfer to glasses.

Boil the tin of condensed milk in a saucepan of water at low temperature for 3 hours. Make sure the water covers the tin all the time it is cooking. Leave the tin to cool before opening it and scraping out the contents. Soak the sheets of gelatine in cold water for about 5 minutes. Stir the sea buckthorn purée, orange juice and sugar until the sugar has dissolved. Heat a little of the purée and melt the sheets of gelatine in it. Mix with the rest of the purée. Fold in the lightly whipped cream, a little at a time. Transfer to an icing bag.

Cover the chocolate cream with toffee cream and top with sea buckthorn purée. Transfer to the fridge to set. Garnish with brownie croutons and chocolate sticks.

Apricots with vanilla cream

10–12 servings or 20 for a smörgåsbord
250 g dried apricots
2½ dl water
2½ tbsp honey
100 g apricot purée
Instant vanilla cream:
½ vanilla pod
1 dl crème fraîche
100 g mascarpone cheese
½ dl icing sugar
Spelt granola:
1½ dl spelt flakes
2 tbsp pumpkin seeds
3 tbsp sunflower seeds
2 tbsp nuts, chopped
2½ tbsp liquid honey

► Chop up the apricots. Simmer them in a saucepan with the water and honey until soft. Mix in the apricot purée and refrigerate. Scrape out the vanilla pod. Mix the seeds with crème fraîche, mascarpone and icing sugar.

Set the oven to 150 °C. Mix all the granola ingredients and stir into a sticky mixture. Tip this out onto a baking tray and roast on the middle shelf of the oven for 30 minutes, stirring every 5 minutes to divide it up. Leave to cool and store in an airtight jar.

Put the apricot cream into glasses or ramekins. Cover with the vanilla cream. (This far you can prepare everything in advance and store it in the fridge.) Sprinkle the vanilla cream with granola before serving.

Småland cheesecake
10–12 servings or 20 for a smörgåsbord
3 litres milk (standard fat content)
1¼ dl white flour
2 tsp cheese rennet
Day 2:
4 dl whipping cream
2½ eggs
1 dl caster sugar
2 small bitter almonds, grated fine
¼ dl sweet almonds, roasted and chopped
► Day 1: Beat 2 dl of the milk, the flour and the rennet together into a smooth mix-

ture. Heat the rest of the milk to 37 ºC. Set aside for about 30 minutes. Stir gently with a large balloon whisk. Remove the cheese mixture with a slotted spoon, transferring it to a tea towel and leaving it to drain through a sieve overnight.

Day 2: Set the oven to 175 ºC. Add the cream, eggs, sugar and the bitter and sweet almonds. Pour the mixture into oven-proof ramekins or one large mould. Bake the cheesecake until it is a nice colour and stays firm when the mould is gently

shaken: this will take 10–12 minutes for ramekins and 20–25 for a large mould.

Bohuslän egg cheese
10–20 servings
4 litres milk
10 eggs
1 litre soured milk (*filmjölk*)
3 dl soured cream (*gräddfil*)
Caster sugar to taste
► Bring the milk gently to the boil. Beat the eggs, soured milk and soured cream together. Stir slowly with a wooden spoon till everything curdles. Scoop

up with a slotted spoon and transfer to a cheese cloth. After it has drained, arrange the curds and sugar in layers in a mould. Refrigerate over-night with a weight on top.
Tip: Alternatively, you can stir a little vanilla cream into the egg cheese and flavour with chopped sweet almonds and a teaspoon or so of Amaretto.

Cloudberry soup

10 servings
1¼ litres water
1¼ dl caster sugar
1 star anise
1 small stick of cinnamon
5 dl cloudberry
1 dl Lakka liqueur
1 tbsp pressed lime
3 g agar agar (powder)/litre
of water

► Day 1: Bring the water, sugar, star anise and cinnamon to the boil. Add the cloudberries. Remove from the heat and leave to cool. Store the saucepan in the fridge overnight.

Day 2: Strain the soup, preferably through a cheese cloth. Save a few cloudberries for garnish. Add Lakka liqueur and pressed lime to taste. Measure the volume.

Bring the soup to the boil with the agar agar. Pour into glasses and garnish with some of the strained-off cloudberries.

Rhubarb dessert

about 12 servings
500 g rhubarb
1½ dl caster sugar
2 cl pressed lemon
2 cl grenadine
½ dl water
Crumble:
2½ dl white flour
1¾ dl caster sugar
60 g cold butter, in cubes
Accompaniment:
2 dl custard

► Peel the rhubarb and slice thinly. Bring the sugar, lemon juice, grenadine and water to the boil. Put in the rhubarb. Cover and remove from the heat. Leave for 30 minutes. Strain off the liquid and stir the rhubarb into a compote.

Set the oven to 175 °C. Mix the flour and sugar in a food processor. Add the butter with the food processor running and keep it running till you have a crumbly dough. Remove this and put out the crumbs on a silicon baking mat. Bake the crumble for 7-8 minutes in the middle of the oven until dry. Crumble it between your hands to divide it into small and slightly larger crumbs. Serve the compote with crumble and custard.

Maltese rice with spiced citrus filets

10–12 servings or 20 for a smörgåsbord
5 dl water
1 tsp salt
1 stick of cinnamon
25 g butter
2½ dl round-grained rice
1¼ litres milk (3% fat content)
2½ dl whipping cream, lightly whipped
about 1 dl icing sugar
Syrup:
1½ dl water
1½ dl caster sugar
3 crushed cardamom seeds
1 star anise
3 cloves
Spiced citrus filets:
1 kg citrus fruits, e.g. orange, blood orange, blood grapefruit

► Bring the water, salt, cinnamon and butter to the boil. Pour in the rice. Bring to the boil, cover and simmer for about 10 minutes, until the liquid has been absorbed. Add the milk, a little at a time, and cook for about 40 minutes. Chill the mixture quickly in iced water. Stir at regular intervals. Refrigerate till the next day.

Bring the syrup ingredients to the boil and cook until the sugar has melted. Leave to cool. Peel the citrus fruits and cut them into filets. Pour the cold syrup over them and leave them to stand in the fridge, preferably overnight.

Fold the cream into the mixture and sweeten to taste with icing sugar. Garnish with citrus filets.

Swedish berry compote

10 servings
600 g assorted fresh berries, e.g. strawberries, raspberries, blackberries, currants
3 tbsp icing sugar
1 tbsp pressed lemon

► Mix 100 g of the berries with the icing sugar and lemon juice. Strain through a fine-meshed strainer. Mix the remaining berries with the sauce – carefully, so as not to mash them. Serve in glasses.

Fig pie

10 servings
3 fresh figs
75 g almond paste
25 g pistachio nuts, chopped
35 g unsalted butter, at room
temperature
1 egg
¾ tbsp white flour
1 drop bitter almond oil
6–10 flan cases
Brushing:
1 egg yolk
► Set the oven to 175 ºC.
Divide the figs and chop them
into little pieces, saving a few
for garnish. Grate the almond
paste on the fine side of the
grater and mix it with the
pistachio nuts and butter. Stir
in the egg, flour and bitter
almond oil. Blend this mixture
with the chopped figs and
transfer to the flan cases. Brush
on top with egg yolk. Bake
in the middle of the oven for
about 7 minutes till golden.
Garnish with a piece of fig on
top.

Chocolate pie

about 12 servings
Chocolate filling:
3 dl whipping cream
1 dl milk (standard fat content)
300 g Manjari Valrhona chocolate
1 egg
1 egg yolk
12 flan cases (see recipe p. 51)
► Set the oven to 150 ºC Bring
the cream and milk to the
boil, remove from the heat
and leave for 1 minute. Chop
the chocolate and put it into a
mixing bowl. Pour the cream
mixture over the chocolate
and stir to a smooth mixture.
Beat the egg and egg yolk
together, and then fold this
into the chocolate mixture.
Transfer the mixture to the flan
cases and bake for 6–7 minutes, depending on size, till it
has just about set. Remove and
put to cool.

Chocolate garnache

100 g dark chocolate 64%
1½ dl whipping cream
35 g glucose
► Chop up the chocolate and
put it into a mixing bowl. Bring
the cream and glucose to the
boil. Pour half this mixture
over the chocolate and stir to a
smooth mixture. Now pour in
the rest and stir to a smooth,
shiny mixture.

Use this glaze for covering
cakes and pastries.

White chocolate cake with spicy pineapple

10–12 servings

325 g white chocolate
275 g butter, at room temperature
183 g egg yolks (about 9 eggs)
380 g whites of egg (about 13 eggs)
225 g caster sugar
140 g white flour
Stewed, caramelised pineapple:
½ pineapple
140 g caster sugar
½ tbsp butter
1 dl water
1 star anise
1 stick of cinnamon
½ tsp rosé pepper
3 crushed green cardamom pods
White chocolate mousse:
100 g white chocolate
250 g whipping cream

► Set the oven to 165 °C. Cut up the chocolate and melt it in the bain-marie. Mix in the butter and egg yolks. Beat the whites of egg and sugar into a meringue. Fold this into the chocolate mixture and sift in the flour. Now pour the mixture into a roasting tin lined with baking paper. Bake in the middle of the oven for 15 minutes. Leave to cool and refrigerate till next day. Cut up in pieces.

Peel and cut up the pineapple. Remove the stalk in the middle. Melt the sugar in a saucepan until it turns golden; do not stir. Add the butter, a knob at a time, and stir carefully so the sugar dissolves. Pour on water and cook until the sugar dissolves. Add the spices and pineapple and simmer gently till the pineapple is soft. Leave to cool, then refrigerate.

Cut up the chocolate and put it in a saucepan together with the cream. Melt over a low flame. Mix with a stick blender. Refrigerate overnight, for at least 6 hours. Whisk the mousse, with the electric whisk at low speed, to the required consistency; if you whisk too rapidly it may curdle.

Serve the cake with stewed pineapple and white chocolate mousse. Garnish with coconut shavings if you like.

Passion fruit pudding and caramel topping

14 servings

325 g passion fruit purée
½ dl pressed orange juice
3¾ dl whipping cream
1 clove
14 egg yolks
2 dl caster sugar
Garnish:
raw sugar

► Bring the passion fruit purée, orange juice, cream and cloves to the boil. Leave to cool. Stir the egg yolks and sugar together. Blend this mixture with the passion fruit syrup. Strain and refrigerate overnight. Set the oven to 150 °C and put a roasting pan of hot water, the water about 1 cm deep, on the middle shelf of the oven. Pour the mixture into oven-proof ramekins and put these in the roasting tin. Cover the ramekins with foil. Bake for about 50 minutes, until the mixture has just set. Remove the foil and put the ramekins to cool in the fridge. Sprinkle with the raw sugar and burn off the surface to make it golden and toffee-like.

Tip. To make a passion fruit pudding, strain the flesh of passion fruits and add 10% sugar to the liquid.

Bread pudding
10–12 servings or 20 for a smörgåsbord
5 dl day-old white bread, cut in cubes
3 tbsp melted butter
1 egg
½ dl caster sugar
50 g almond paste, coarse-grated
3 dl milk

½ dl chopped apricots
½ dl chopped dried figs
½ dl yellow raisins
½ dl roasted sweet almonds, chopped

▶ Set the oven to 180 ºC and put in a bowl of water. Mix the bread and butter. Mix the eggs, sugar, almond paste and milk. Combine this with the bread. Grease an oven-proof dish. Fill it with alternate layers of bread, almonds, apricots, figs and raisins. Bake for about 30 minutes in the middle of the oven in a bain-marie.

Sea buckthorn yoghurt ice cream

10 servings
¾ sheet gelatine
140 g caster sugar
110 g water
250 g sea buckthorn purée (containing 10% sugar)
150 g yoghurt naturel

▶ Soak the gelatine in cold water for 5 minutes. Boil sugar and water for 5 minutes to make a syrup. Leave to cool slightly. Remove the gelatine from the water, melt it in the syrup and fold in the sea buckthorn purée. Leave to cool. Stir the yoghurt into the fruit purée, making sure there are no lumps remaining. Store the ice cream mixture in the fridge overnight to bring out the flavours.

Run the mixture in an ice cream maker, preferably on the day of serving.

Tip. This ice cream recipe also works with other flavours; just substitute another flavour – raspberries or cherries, for example – for the purée.

Coffee ice cream

10 servings
½ sheet gelatine
250 g whipping cream
250 g milk
25 g glucose
120 g egg yolk
65 g caster sugar
60 g dark muscovado sugar
½ dl whole coffee beans
1 tbsp coffee liqueur

▶ Day 1: Soak the gelatine in cold water for 5 minutes. Bring the cream, milk and glucose to the boil. Beat the egg yolks, sugar and muscovado sugar fluffy. Whisk the warm cream mixture into the egg yolks. Return the mixture to the saucepan and heat to 82 °C, stirring continuously with a wooden spoon. Remove the gelatine from the water and melt it in the ice cream mixture. Strain and fold in the coffee beans. Chill instantly in an ice bath. Store the ice cream mixture in the fridge overnight to bring out the flavours.

Day 2. Fold in the coffee liqueur, strain and process in the ice cream maker.

Vanilla ice cream

10 servings
½ sheet gelatine
1 vanilla pod
250 g whipping cream
250 g milk
25 g glucose
120 g egg yolk
125 g sugar

▶ Day 1: Soak the gelatine in cold water for 5 minutes. Split the vanilla pod and scrape out the seeds. Bring the cream, milk, glucose, vanilla pod and vanilla seeds to the boil. Beat the egg yolks and sugar fluffy. Whisk the warm cream mixture into the egg yolks. Return the mixture to the saucepan and heat to 82 °C, stirring continuously with a wooden spoon. Remove the gelatine from the water and melt it in the ice cream mixture. Strain and chill instantly in an ice bath, returning the vanilla pod to the mixture. Store in the fridge overnight to bring out the flavours.

Day 2. Strain and process in the ice cream maker.

Rice porridge
8 servings
2 dl round-grained porridge rice
½ tsp salt
1 tbsp caster sugar
6–8 cm stick of cinnamon
2 dl water
8 dl milk (standard fat content)

► Bring the rice, salt, sugar, cinnamon and water to the boil. Reduce the heat to simmering. Cover and cook for 10 minutes. Heat the milk in a saucepan. Dilute the porridge with the milk, a little at a time, stirring at regular intervals to keep it from burning. Cover and simmer for 45–50 minutes.

Blueberry milk
12 servings
1 litre fresh blueberries
3 tbsp caster sugar
1 litre cold milk
► Mix the blueberries carefully with the caster sugar and put them in glasses. Pour on the cold milk and serve immediately.

Strawberries in milk
10 servings
1 litre strawberries
2 tbsp caster sugar
1 litre milk, 3% fat content
► Hull and wipe the strawberries. Quarter them and mix with the sugar. Transfer to a bowl and pour on the milk just before serving.

Saffron pancake

20 servings

2 sachets (0.5 g each) of saffron
2 tbsp punch
6–7 dl rice porridge (see recipe p. 202)
100 g almond paste, grated
about 1 dl honey
½ tsp ground cinnamon
5 eggs
½ dl flaked almonds

► Set the oven to 175 °C. Dissolve the saffron in the punch and mix it into the porridge together with the grated almond paste and honey. Add cinnamon to taste. Beat the eggs and mix them into the porridge. Grease an oven dish, about 20 x 4 cm, and line it with dried breadcrumbs. Pour in the mixture and sprinkle the almonds over it. Bake in the bottom half of the oven for about 30 minutes, until the pancake has set. Cloudberry preserve makes a good garnish.

Cloudberry preserve

8–10 servings

250 g frozen cloudberries
125 g caster sugar
2 tbsp Lakka cloudberry liqueur

► Stir sugar and Lakka liqueur into the cloudberries and keep stirring till the sugar has dissolved, but stir carefully, so that the cloudberries do not disintegrate. Leave to stand for about 1 hour.

Berries with yoghurt and caramel muesli
10 servings
1.4 dl rolled oats
2 tbsp chopped hazelnuts
2½ tbsp liquid honey
3 dl yoghurt naturel, 10%
500 g assorted berries, e.g. strawberries, blueberries, wild strawberries, raspberries

► Set the oven to 150 ºC. Mix the rolled oats, hazelnuts and honey together. Pour the mixture onto a baking tray and bake in the middle of the oven for 30 minutes. Stir the muesli every 5 minutes, to spread the grains. Leave to cool and store in an airtight tin.

Mix the yoghurt, fresh berries and caramel muesli together in a bowl.

Swedish berries threaded on grass stalks

10 servings

300 g assorted berries, e.g. wild strawberries and blueberries

10 stalks of timothy grass

3 dl yoghurt naturel, 10%

½ dl caster sugar

► Thread the berries on the straws in random order. Stir the yoghurt and sugar into a smooth cream. Serve the skewered berries with the sugar yoghurt.

Wild raspberries with lemon cream

12 servings
1 sheet of gelatine
¾ dl pressed lemon
1½ dl caster sugar
100 g unsalted butter
2 eggs
2 tbsp yoghurt naturel, 10%
12 flan cases (see recipe p. 51)
1 litre raspberries

► Soak the sheet of gelatine in cold water for about 5 minutes. Mix the lemon juice, sugar, butter and egg together in a saucepan. Cover and simmer until you have a smooth cream. Remove from the heat. Remove the sheet of gelatine from the water and melt it in the cream. Strain and refrigerate. Fold the yoghurt into the lemon cream.

Put lemon cream on the bottom of each flan case and garnish with a raspberry on top.

Blueberry pie

12 servings
500 g blueberries
½ dl caster sugar
1 tbsp Maizena cornflour starch
10–12 flan cases (see recipe p. 51)
Crumbly pastry:
2½ dl white flour
1¾ dl caster sugar
60 g cold butter, diced

► Set the oven to 175 ºC. Mix the blueberries, sugar and cornflour starch carefully together. Put to one side. Mix the flour and sugar in a food processor. Add the butter and keep the food processor running till you have a crumbly dough.

Put the blueberries into the flan cases and crumble the dough over them. Bake in the middle of the oven for about 7 minutes, until the pies have just about changed colour. Serve with custard.

Pie of apples fried in sugar

12 servings
500 g firm green apples
1 tbsp pressed lemon
1 tbsp butter
1¾ dl caster sugar
12 flan cases (see recipe p. 51)

► Peel and de-core the apples and cut them into small cubes. Put them in cold water with the lemon juice. Remove them and put them to drain on a tea towel. Melt the butter in a frying pan until it is nearly golden. Put in the apple cubes and fry them carefully for 1 minute. Sprinkle with the sugar and shake round till the sugar has melted and formed a crust round the apple cubes. Transfer immediately to a baking tray to cool. Put the apple cubes into the flan cases. Pour on a little of the apple juices remaining in the pan.

Custard

10–20 servings
2¼ dl whipping cream
4 dl milk (standard fat content)
1 vanilla pod, split down the middle
1.4 dl caster sugar
5 egg yolks

► Bring the cream, milk and vanilla pod to the boil. Beat the sugar and egg yolks till fluffy. Beat the warm cream-and-milk mixture into this. Return the saucepan to the cooker and keep stirring till the temperature reaches 83ºC. Strain and cool quickly in ice water or the fridge.

Coffee, biscuits and confectionery

A simple but worthy conclusion to the smörgåsbord! Coffee has become part of the life and soul of the Swedish nation – waking us up in the morning, keeping us on our toes for the rest of the day and rounding off our mealtimes. Time was when coffee was thought to be sheer depravity and the enemy of amorous enterprise…

But now we know better. Swedes and Finns are the world's best coffee drinkers, downing upwards of 150 litres a year per capita. We have chosen to round off with coffee, seven different cakes and biscuits, and confectionary.

Marzipan loaf

2 loaves

300 g marzipan
150 g dark chocolate

► Divide the marzipan in 2 pieces and roll into oblong loaves. Put these on a wire rack. Melt the chocolate in a bain-marie or microwave. Brush the marzipan loaves with the chocolate. Leave to set at room temperature. For a smoother result, raise the chocolate to room temperature first.

Mint kisses

30–40 kisses

270 g caster sugar
100 g water
1 tbsp glucose
8 drops peppermint oil
40 g melted chocolate

► Melt the sugar and glucose in the water in a saucepan and simmer to 120 ºC. Keep the lid slightly off the saucepan, so the syrup will not stick to the sides. Add the peppermint oil. Pour the mixture onto a silicon baking sheet or a sheet of baking paper. Stir the mixture to aerate it and turn it white. Transfer to a mixing bowl and heat over a bain-marie. Transfer, a dob at a time, to a silicon baking sheet or a sheet of baking paper. Leave to set. Melt the chocolate in a bain-marie or the micro and release a small drop of chocolate onto each kiss.

Chocolate truffle

40 pieces

110 g caster sugar
310 g whipping cream
375 g dark chocolate, 64%
105 g butter
1 orange, grated zest of
4 cl Grand Marnier
Garnish:
about 2 dl cocoa

► Bring the sugar and cream to the boil and put aside for about 1 minute. Put the chocolate into a food processor and chop it quickly. Pour on the warm cream mixture with the machine running. Add the butter, a knob at a time, followed by the orange zest and liqueur.

Pour the truffle mixture into a plastic-lined tin and leave it to set at room temperature. Now put it in the fridge for about 30 minutes. Remove and shape into 40 balls. Roll these in cocoa. Store in the fridge and serve at room temperature.

Johanna's grandma's caramels

about 60 caramels

4½ dl whipping cream
4½ dl caster sugar
1¾ dl golden syrup
½ tbsp cocoa
1 tbsp butter

► Mix the cream, sugar, syrup, cocoa and half the butter in a saucepan. Simmer gently to 122 ºC. Add the remaining butter. Pour the caramel onto a sheet of baking paper. Leave to set for at least 8 hours at room temperature. Cut the caramels to the required shape and wrap them in twists of greaseproof paper.

Blackberry marmalade

about 100 pieces

500 g blackberry juice
100 g apple purée
850 g caster sugar
20 g pectin
150 g glucose
15 g citric acid
1 tbsp vodka
Garnish:
caster sugar

► Bring the blackberry juice and apple purée to the boil and skim it. Mix the sugar and pectin thoroughly. Stir the sugar into the warm juice together with the glucose. Boil to 107 ºC. Dissolve the citric acid in the vodka and whisk into the warm purée – gently, so as not to form any bubbles. Transfer to a plastic-lined dish and leave to cool at room temperature. Cut the marmalade into pieces and dredge them in caster sugar before serving.

Raspberry marmalade
about 100 pieces
500 g raspberry purée
100 g apple purée
850 g caster sugar
20 g pectin
150 g glucose
15 g citric acid
15 g vodka
Garnish:
caster sugar
► Bring the raspberry and apple purée to the boil and skim it. Mix the sugar and pectin thoroughly, then fold into the warm purée together with the glucose. Boil to 107 ºC. Dissolve the citric acid in the vodka and whisk it into the warm purée – carefully, to avoid any bubbles. Transfer to a plastic-lined bowl, about 15 x 25 cm, and leave to cool at room temperature.
Cut the marmalade into pieces and dredge these in caster sugar when serving.

Sea buckthorn marmalade
about 100 pieces
500 g sea buckthorn juice
100 g apple purée
150 g glucose
850 g caster sugar
20 g pectin
15 g citric acid
1 tbsp vodka
Garnish:
caster sugar
► Bring the sea buckthorn juice and apple purée to the boil and skim it. Mix the sugar and pectin thoroughly. Stir the sugar into the warm juice together with the glu-cose. Boil to 107 ºC. Dissolve the citric acid in the vodka and whisk into the warm purée – gently, so as not to form any bubbles. Transfer to a plastic-lined dish and leave to cool at room temperature. Cut the marmalade into piec-es and dredge them in caster sugar before serving.

Almond chocolate
about 30 pieces
250 g dark chocolate, 64 %
1 dl whipping cream
80 g solid honey
50 g unsalted butter, cut into cubes
1 tbsp praliné (hazelnut paste)
100 g flaked roasted sweet almonds
► Chop the dark chocolate and put it in a mixing bowl. Bring the whipping cream and honey to the boil and then pour it over the choco-late, stirring continuously. Stir in the butter, praliné and almonds. Transfer to a 1½ litre raised mould, e.g. an oblong loaf tin, lined with plastic foil. Leave to set at room temperature for about 2 hours. Cut the chocolate in pieces.

Chocolate balls
about 25 balls
150 g unsalted butter, at room temperature
2 dl caster sugar
3½ dl rolled oats
1 dl coconut flakes
4½ tbsp cocoa
2 tbsp strong coffee
1 tbsp brandy
Garnish:
coconut flakes
► Beat the butter and sugar to a smooth mixture. Add the rolled oats and coconut. Stir in the coffee and brandy. Transfer the dough to the fridge for 10 minutes. Roll into little balls and dredge these in coconut.

Ginger snap balls
See recipe page 226.

For that genuine Christmas feeling, the yuletide smörgås-bord is often decorated with marzipan figures, gingerbread houses and other seasonal embellishments.

Lingonberry and almond rusks

about 80 rusks

100 g soft butter
1¼ dl caster sugar
½ dl golden syrup
2 oranges, grated zest of
1 egg
70 g sweet almonds
40 g dried lingonberries
30 g chocolate, chopped
275 g white flour
½ tsp baking powder
¼ tsp bicarb
¼ tsp salt
2 tsp crushed coriander seeds
1–2 drops bitter almond oil
2 tsp vanilla sugar

► Set the oven to 175 ºC. Stir the butter, sugar and syrup together into a fluffy mixture. Stir in the orange zest and egg. Add the other ingredients and work into a smooth dough. Shape this into 4 flat rolls. Bake in the middle of the oven for 12–14 minutes. Remove and leave to cool. Cut the rolls into pieces about 1 cm wide and return them to the baking tray with the cut surface uppermost. Bake for another 10 minutes or so, until the rusks are dry.

Store the rusks in an airtight tin after they have cooled.

Madeleines with orange
For the best results, prepare the mixture a day in advance.
25–30 cakes
2 large eggs
5 tbsp caster sugar
2 tsp Demerara sugar
1½ dl white flour
1 tsp baking powder
1 orange, grated zest of

90 g melted butter
Garnish:
icing sugar
► Set the oven to 175 ºC. Beat the eggs, sugar and Demerara sugar together. Sift in the flour and baking powder. Fold in the orange zest and butter and beat the mixture till it stiffens slightly. Transfer to an

icing bag and squirt into small, well-greased cases. Bake in the middle of the oven for about 5 minutes. Tip the Madeleines out and sift icing sugar over them before serving.

Doughnuts with orange and green cheese

about 30 doughnuts

75 g butter
100 g milk
285 g white flour
30 g caster sugar
25 g yeast
1 egg

Frying medium:
corn oil
Garnish:
cinnamon and caster sugar
Filling:
300 g green cheese
50 g icing sugar
1 orange, grated zest of
1 tbsp Grand Marnier

► Melt the butter and mix it with the milk. Heat to 37 ºC. Mix with the white flour, sugar, crumbled yeast and egg. Run this in a small dough mixer or food processor for 7-9 minutes, till you have a supple dough. Shape the dough into 30 little balls and store them in the fridge for about 2 hours. Remove them and put them to prove (rise) for 30 minutes. Heat the oil to 180 ºC. Deep-fry the balls until they are golden brown, then put them to drain on kitchen tissue. Roll them in cinnamon and caster sugar.

Mix the filling ingredients. Transfer to an icing bag with a small spout and fill the cream into the balls.

Toffee

about 70 small pieces

2 dl whipping cream
2 dl golden syrup
2 dl caster sugar
1 tsp vanilla sugar
2 tbsp butter
¾ dl sweet almonds and pistachio nuts, chopped

► Mix the cream, syrup, sugar, vanilla sugar and butter together in a saucepan. Boil without covering, stirring occasionally, until the temperature reaches 124 ºC or until the mixture passes the ball test: pour a few drops of it into ice-cold water and roll into a ball, which must be firm to hard. Remove the mixture from the heat and leave it for 15–30 minutes. Transfer to little paper cases and sprinkle with the chopped nuts. Leave to set. A word of advice. Don't try doubling this recipe. Make 2 batches instead.

Dreams

Makes 125–150
240 g + 60 g butter
360 g caster sugar
360 g white flour
6 g hartshorn
2 g baking powder
► Set the oven to 150 °C. Brown 240 g butter. Strain off the dark sediment and leave the butter to cool. Mix the browned butter with 60 g fresh butter. Sift in the other ingredients and mix quickly into quite a crumbly dough, e.g. in a food processor with a plastic knife. Shape the dough into little balls weighing 8–10 g each. Put them on baking trays lined with baking paper. Bake in the middle of the oven for 6–8 minutes. Leave to cool. Store in a lidded tin or jar.

Chocolate slices

Makes 40–50
260 g white flour
40 g cocoa
180 g cold butter
180 g caster sugar
Brushing:
½ egg
Decorating:
pearl sugar
► Set the oven to 165 °C. Sift the flour and cocoa together. Mix the butter and sugar. Add the other ingredients and mix quickly into a dough, e.g. in a food processor with a plastic knife. Roll into lengths about 2½ cm across and put these on baking trays lined with baking paper. Flatten them with your hand. Brush with whisked egg and sprinkle with pearl sugar. Bake in the middle of the oven for 8–10 minutes. Cut the lengths into pieces about 2 cm wide. Leave them to cool, then store them in biscuit tins.

Jam biscuits

Makes 40–50
360 g cold butter
120 g icing sugar
400 g white flour
White of ½ egg
Filling:
raspberry or strawberry jam
► Mix the butter and icing sugar together. Add the flour and white of egg and mix quickly into a dough. Shape the dough into rolls about 2½ cm in diameter. Put these in the fridge to set. Set the oven to 165 °C. Cut into pieces about 1 cm wide and put out on a baking sheet with the cut surface uppermost. Press a small hole with your thumb and squirt in a little jam. Bake in the middle of the oven for about 8 minutes, until they have turned a nice colour. Leave them to cool, then store them in a biscuit tin.

.

Vanilla horns

Makes 40–50
325 g white flour
200 g butter
2 tbsp real vanilla sugar
Decorating:
caster sugar
► Set the oven to 165 °C. Run all the ingredients in a food processor with a plastic knife till you have a supple dough. Divide this into 10 g pieces and roll them into balls. Shape the balls into horns. Put them onto a baking tray lined with baking paper. Bake in the middle of the oven for about 8 minutes, until they have turned a nice colour. On removing them from the oven, dip them in sugar immediately, to make sure it sticks. Leave them to cool, then store them in a biscuit tin.

French ginger snaps

Makes 40–50
195 g white flour
12 g crushed cinnamon
4 g crushed ginger
3 g crushed cloves
2½ g bicarb
100 g butter
80 g caster sugar
75 g golden syrup
100 g flaked almonds
► Sift the flour and spices together. Mix the butter, sugar and syrup together in a food processor with a plastic knife. Add the flour mixture and work quickly into a supple dough. Add the almonds. Press out the dough into an oblong sponge tin, 1½ litre, lined on the bottom with baking paper. Leave in the fridge to set. Set the oven to 165 °C. Remove the dough from the tin and cut it into lengths of about 3 x 5 cm. Cut these into thin snaps and put them onto a baking tray lined with baking paper. Bake in the middle of the oven for about 8 minutes. The leftovers from cutting up the dough can be kneaded together, stored in the fridge and later cut into thin snaps and baked. Leave the ginger snaps to cool, then store them in a biscuit tin.

Cinnamon sticks

Makes 40–50
250 g butter
250 g white flour
½ dl whipping cream
Brushing:
egg
Decorating:
caster sugar mixed with crushed cinnamon
► Run all the ingredients in a food processor with a plastic knife till you have a smooth dough. Flatten this out on a baking tray lined with baking paper and store in the fridge overnight to set. Roll the dough to a thickness of about ½ cm. Brush with beaten egg and sprinkle overall with "cinnamon sugar". Put to freeze in the freezer. Set the oven to 165 °C. Cut the sheet into lengths 8 cm wide and then cut these into sticks 1½ cm long. Transfer to a baking tray lined with baking paper and bake in the middle of the oven for 8–10 minutes, till the sticks are a nice colour. Leave them to cool, then store in a biscuit tin.

Warning! These cookies are very brittle indeed, so be careful when putting them in the tin.

Crunch

Makes 40–50
210 g butter at room temperature
150 g caster sugar
35 g black treacle
300 g white flour
14 g crushed ginger
7 g bicarb
► Set the oven to 165 °C. Mix the butter, sugar and treacle into a smooth batter. Sift in the dry ingredients and mix rapidly into a smooth dough, using a food processor with a plastic knife. Shape the dough into rolls about 2 cm in diameter. Transfer to a baking tray lined with baking paper and flatten. Bake in the middle of the oven for about 8 minutes, till the cookies are a nice colour. On removing them from the oven, cut them up immediately into pieces about 2 cm wide. Leave them to cool, then store in a biscuit tin.

Ginger snap balls

Makes about 24

2 eggs
1¼ dl icing sugar
1 tbsp real vanilla sugar
4 tbsp cocoa
250 g ginger snaps
75 g butter
2 tbsp Grand Marnier
Garnish:
100 g ginger snaps

► Whisk the eggs together with the icing sugar, vanilla sugar and cocoa into a smooth batter. Run the ginger snaps in a food processor to make crumbs of them. Melt the butter. Mix the egg batter and ginger snap crumbs, butter and liqueur together. Cover with plastic foil and refrigerate overnight.

Run the ginger snaps for the garnish in a food processor. Shape the dough into balls and roll these in the ginger snap crumbs. Store in the fridge.

Ginger snaps

Makes about 150

435 g white flour
250 g golden syrup
150 g butter, at room temperature
75 g caster sugar
1 egg
1 tsp bicarb
½ tbsp crushed cinnamon
½ tbsp crushed cloves
1 tsp crushed ginger

► Run all the ingredients in a food processor for 2–3 minutes until you have a smooth dough. Wrap this in plastic foil and refrigerate for about 2 hours. Set the oven to 200 ºC. Get out a little of the dough at a time, roll it thin (about 1.5 mm) on a floured worktop and stamp out ginger snaps with cutters. Bake in the middle of the oven for 5–7 minute, until they are a nice golden colour.

Coconut pyramids with saffron and pistachio nuts

Makes 50–60 small ones

50 g butter
0.5 g saffron
2 eggs
1 dl caster sugar
about 5 dl coconut flakes
(nearly 200 g)
3 tbs pistachio nuts, chopped
Garnish:
100 g white chocolate
1 tbsp pistachio nuts, chopped

► Set the oven to 175 ºC. Melt the butter and mix in the saffron. Stir the eggs and sugar together. Add the coconut, pistachio nuts and butter. Leave to swell for 10 minutes. Shape small pyramids between teaspoons and place them on baking trays lined with baking paper. Bake in the middle of the oven for 6–8 minutes. Leave to cool.

Apple and blackberry muffins
Makes 25
150 g melted butter
2 dl caster sugar
3 eggs
2½ dl white flour
1 tsp baking powder
0.5 g saffron
2 apples, or else 25 blackberries
Garnish:
3 tbsp icing sugar
► Set the oven to 225 ºC. Stir the butter and sugar together. Work in the eggs, one at a time. Mix the flour, baking powder and saffron. Sift this mixture into the batter and stir till smooth. Use an icing bag to squirt the batter into paper cases on a baking tray. Peel the apples and cut them up. Stick a piece of apple or a blackberry into each muffin. Bake in the middle of the oven for 7–8 minutes.

Almond mussels
about 40 mussels
50 g almond paste
30 g sweet almonds, crushed
240 g butter, at room temperature
1 dl caster sugar
5 dl white flour
a few drops of bitter almond oil
► Blend the almond paste, almonds and butter into a smooth mixture. Add the sugar, flour and bitter almond oil, mixing rapidly into a dough. Store overnight in the fridge. Roll the pastry thin and line fluted patty tins (moulds) with it. Set the oven to 200 ºC and bake the mussels for 6-8 minutes, until golden brown. Remove them from the moulds when they have cooled a little.

Christmas crullers
about 35 crullers
1 egg
1 egg yolk
¾ dl golden syrup
20 g melted butter
2 tbsp whipping cream
not quite 4 dl white flour
1 tsp baking powder
½ lemon, grated zest of
Frying medium:
corn oil
Garnish:
caster sugar
crushed cinnamon
► Mix the egg, egg yolk and syrup in a mixing bowl. Add the remaining ingredients and work into a supple dough. Store in the fridge for at least 1 hour. Roll the dough thin and cut it into diagonal strips with a pastry wheel. Make a slit in the middle. Pull one pointed end through this and twist into a screw shape. Heat the oil to 165 ºC. Mix the sugar and cinnamon together. Deep-fry the crullers until they are golden brown. Put them to drain on kitchen tissue and then dredge them in sugar and cinnamon.

Marshmallows
50–60 pieces
75 g gelatine powder
1¼ dl cold water
5 dl caster sugar
1½ dl golden syrup
4 tbsp water
¼ tsp salt
Garnish:
coconut or icing sugar
► Mix the gelatine powder
and cold water together and
leave for 10 minutes. Mix the
sugar, syrup and water in a
saucepan. Bring to the boil and
keep it boiling vigorously for 1
minute. Fold into the gelatine
while still warm and whisk for
2 minutes. Pour the mixture
into an oiled oven dish, about
15 x 25 cm, and cover with
plastic foil. Smooth the surface
and leave to set at room temperature. Cut up in pieces and
roll them in coconut or icing
sugar.

Granola crunch
25–30 servings
100 g dark chocolate
granola (see recipe p. 207)
► Melt the chocolate and stir in granola according to taste. Pour onto a baking tray lined with plastic foil. Leave to set at room temperature. Break into suitably sized pieces before serving.

Miniature Swiss roll with lingonberry filling and lingonberry dip

25–30 slices

4 egg yolks
1½ dl caster sugar
4 whites of egg
2 dl white flour
1½ tsp crushed cinnamon
½ tsp crushed ginger
Garnish:
caster sugar
Filling:
200 g lingonberry juice
50 g pear purée
2 dl caster sugar
Lingonberry dip:
2 dl yoghurt naturel, 10 %
½ dl icing sugar
2 tbsp mashed lingonberries

► Set the oven to 225ºC. Beat the egg yolks and half the sugar together. Beat the whites of egg and the rest of the sugar into a firm meringue mixture. Blend this and the egg yolk mixture carefully together and gently fold in the flour, mixed with the spices. Spread the mixture on baking paper in a roasting tin. Bake on the middle shelf of the oven for 4–5 minutes until pale brown. Sprinkle with the sugar. Put a sheet of baking paper on top and turn over. Leave to cool, then store in the freezer.

Mix the lingonberry juice and pear purée with the sugar. Spread the lingonberry purée on the bottom and roll up. Cut into small pieces and put a cocktail stick into each one for easier handling.

Stir the yoghurt, icing sugar and mashed lingonberries together and serve with the miniature Swiss roll.

Accompaniments

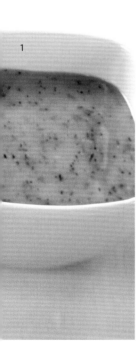

1. Mustard-and-dill-sauce ("head waiter's sauce")

10 servings
1 dl Swedish mustard
1 dl caster sugar
4 tbsp white wine vinegar
2 dl oil, e.g. grape seed oil
1 tbsp honey
1 tsp salt
2–3 tsp cold filter coffee
2 dl chopped dill
► Mix the mustard, sugar and vinegar. Add the oil, first a drop at a time and then in a fine jet, whisking all the time. Add honey, salt and coffee to taste. Add the chopped dill when serving.

2. Sea buckthorn mustard

10–20 servings
1 dl brown mustard seeds
1 dl yellow mustard seeds
just under 1 dl water
1 dl sea buckthorn juice (or sea buckthorn run in the food processor and strained afterwards)
1 tbsp apple cider vinegar
2 tbsp golden syrup
2 tbsp liquid honey
2 tsp brandy
1 tsp salt
1 dl Dijon mustard
½ dl oil, e.g. grape seed oil
► Mix all the ingredients together in a food processor. Transfer to jars with close-fitting lids. Store the mustard in a cool, dark place. Let it stand for a week before serving, to bring out the flavour.

3. Miso and cloudberry mustard sauce

10–20 servings
Sweet miso paste:
1 dl Lakka, cloudberry liqueur
1 dl mirin
1¾ dl caster sugar
3 dl white miso paste
mustard sauce:
1 tsp Colman's mustard powder or Japanese mustard powder
2 tsp warm water
300 g sweet miso paste, see above
2 tbsp rice vinegar
► Stir the Lakka, mirin and sugar together until all the sugar has dissolved. Fold in the miso paste. Dissolve the mustard powder in the warm water and mix with the sweet miso and rice wine vinegar.

4. Calvados mustard

10–20 servings
1 dl brown mustard seeds
½ dl water
½ dl good-quality Calvados
½ dl liquid honey
½ dl Dijon mustard
1½ dl Swedish mustard
2 pinches of salt
► Pound the mustard seeds in a mortar, then heat them in a saucepan together with the water, Calvados and honey. Remove from the heat and leave to cool. Add the other ingredients and leave in a cool place. Store for a week, so as to bring out the flavours.

5. Strong honey mustard

10–20 servings
2 tbsp Colman's mustard powder
2 tbsp water
1 dl Dijon mustard
1 dl liquid acacia honey
1 tsp apple cider vinegar
2 pinches of salt
► Stir the mustard powder and water together, then mix in the other ingredients. Transfer to jars with close-fitting lids. Store the mustard in a cool place, for a week if possible, so as to bring out the flavour.

6. Coarse mustard sauce

10–20 servings
1 dl coarse Dijon mustard
2 tbsp Dijon mustard
3 tbsp caster sugar
3 tbsp apple cider vinegar
2 dl oil, e.g. grape seed oil
salt
► Mix the mustard, sugar and vinegar together. Add the oil, first a drop at a time and then in a fine jet, whisking all the time. Add salt to taste.

7. Espresso mustard sauce

10–20 servings
½ dl Swedish mustard
½ dl Dijon mustard
1¼ dl caster sugar
1 tbsp white wine vinegar
1 tsp salt
2½ dl oil, e.g. grape seed oil
3 tbsp espresso or strong coffee
2 tbsp Demerara sugar
► Mix the mustard, Dijon mustard, sugar, vinegar and salt. Add the oil, first a drop at a time and then in a fine jet, whisking vigorously all the time. Add the espresso, followed by Demerara sugar to taste.

1. Granny Smith stewed apples

10–20 servings

10 sharp apples, e.g. Granny Smith
2 tbsp Calvados
1 tsp citric acid
1 lemon, pressed juice of
½ dl caster sugar
1 tbsp flat-leafed parsley, chopped small

► Peel and de-core the apples and cut them into equal-sized pieces. Put these into a saucepan along with the Calvados, citric acid and lemon juice. Simmer, stirring all the time, until mushy. Add the sugar and let it melt. This will make the stewed apple slightly transparent. Add the parsley when serving.

2. Spicy figs

10–20 servings

16 fresh figs
500 g firm pears
150 g raw sugar
1 dl white wine vinegar
1 tsp salt
2 bay leaves
1 tsp crushed black peppercorns
½ tsp crushed coriander seeds

► Quarter the figs. Peel, de-core and chop the pears. Put the chopped pears into a saucepan – not an aluminium one. Add the sugar, vinegar, salt and bay leaves. Bring to the boil, stirring all the time. Boil almost dry before adding the figs and spices. Cover and cook gently over a low flame for 30 minutes, stirring at regular intervals.

Transfer to a clean glass jar and store in the fridge. Your spicy figs will keep for about 2 months.

3. Uncooked, stirred lingonberries with a sting in their tail

10–20 servings

200 g frozen lingonberries
½ dl red wine vinegar
1½ dl caster sugar
1 tbsp chopped fresh ginger

► Stir all the ingredients together, but carefully, so as not to crush the berries. Refrigerate overnight.

4. Chutney with apricots, orange and cloves

10–20 servings

200 g dried apricots
1 orange
1 red chilli, e.g. Spanish pepper
½ dl white wine vinegar
10 cloves
½ dl caster sugar
1 stick of cinnamon
2 star aniseeds

► Cut the apricots into strips. Peel the orange and slice it thinly. De-seed the chilli and cut it into strips. Put all the ingredients into a saucepan and cook over a low flame for about 1½ hours. The chutney is ready when the apricots have softened and the sauce thickened. Dilute with a little water if the sauce is too thick.

5. Cumberland sauce with figs

10–20 servings

100 g dried figs
½ dl red wine
1 dl red port
½ tsp mustard powder
1 pinch of ginger
1 cinnamon stick
5 cloves
2 tbsp fig vinegar
2½ dl red currant jelly
1 orange, grated zest and pressed juice of
½ lemon, grated zest and pressed juice of

► Cut the figs into strips after removing their stalks. Put the figs in a saucepan. Add the wine, port, spices and fig vinegar. Simmer, uncovered, for about 10 minutes. Strain the red currant jelly through a sieve. Mix the jelly and lemon zest into the fig sauce. Dilute with the orange and lemon juice. Refrigerate.

Herb mayonnaise

10–20 servings

2 dl mayonnaise
1 tbsp Dijon mustard
1 tsp chopped parsley
1 tsp chopped basil
1 tsp chopped tarragon
salt
white pepper

▶ Mix all the ingredients and add salt and pepper to taste.

Smoked mayonnaise

10–20 servings

3 dl rapeseed oil
6 stalks of thyme
100 g smoked side pork, diced
1 clove of garlic, peeled
2 egg yolks
1 tbsp Dijon mustard
1 tsp white wine vinegar
water, if needed
salt, white pepper

▶ Pour the oil into a saucepan together with the thyme, pork and garlic. Simmer gently for 30 minutes. Strain the oil and put it to cool.

Beat the egg yolks, mustard and vinegar together till fluffy. Add the strained oil, a drop at a time, whisking vigorously. Dilute with water if the mayonnaise gets too thick. Add salt and pepper to taste. Serve with poached salmon.

Beetroot salad

10–20 servings
400 g pickled beetroot, diced
1 apple, e.g. Granny Smith, diced
1 dl mayonnaise
1 dl crème fraîche
2 tbsp white wine vinegar
1 tbsp Dijon mustard
1 tbsp grated horseradish
1 orange, grated zest of
salt, white pepper

► Mix all the ingredients and add salt and white pepper to taste. The vinegar in the salad has the effect of heightening the colour of the beetroot.

Pressed cucumber

10–20 servings

1 dl distilled vinegar (*ättika*, 12% strength)
2 dl caster sugar
3 dl water
1 tsp yellow mustard seeds
1 cucumber
2 tbsp chopped curly leaf parsley

► Stir the *ättika*, sugar and water until the sugar has dissolved. Mix in the mustard seeds. Cut the cucumber into thin slices and put these into the liquid. Put a plate or some other heavy object on top of the cucumber and refrigerate for about 2 hours or overnight. Stir in the parsley before serving.

Sharp sauce

10–20 servings

1 tbsp Dijon mustard
2 raw egg yolks
2 boiled eggs, chopped small
2 dl rapeseed oil
2 tsp caster sugar
2 tbsp white wine vinegar
salt
pepper
2 tbsp chopped dill
2 tbsp whipping cream, lightly whipped

► Mix the mustard, egg yolks and boiled eggs together in a mixing bowl. All the ingredients must be at the same temperature. Add the oil to the egg mixture, a drop at a time, whisking vigorously. Fold in the sugar and vinegar. Add salt and pepper to taste. Add the dill and fold in the cream. Leave in the fridge for at least an hour, to bring out the flavour.

Mimosa salad

10–20 servings

4 tbsp mayonnaise
1 dl whipping cream
2 tbsp pressed lemon juice
1 small apple, diced
1 small pear, diced
2 slices of fresh pineapple, diced
10 seedless grapes, halved
2 celery stalks, peeled and diced
1 boiled egg
salt
pepper

► Mix the mayonnaise, cream and lemon juice together. Fold in the apple, pear, pineapple, grapes and celery. Shell the egg and divide it in two. Chop the white and mix it into the salad. Add salt and pepper to taste. Press the yolk through a sieve and garnish the salad with it.

Horseradish cream

10–20 servings

2 dl whipping cream
1 tbsp grated horseradish or more, as preferred
1 tsp Dijon mustard
salt

► Whip the cream lightly and fold in the grated horseradish and mustard. Add a little salt to taste.

Mackmyra mustard

10–20 servings

1 dl brown mustard seeds
1 dl water
½ dl Mackmyra whisky
½ dl golden syrup
½ dl liqud honey
3 tbsp cider vinegar
1 dl Dijon mustard
2 dl coarse mustard, e.g. cider vinegar
2 pinches of salt

► Pound the mustard seeds in a mortar. Heat them up in a saucepan with the water, whisky, golden syrup and honey. Remove from the heat and leave to cool. Add the other ingredients and store in a cool place. Leave for a couple of days or so, while the flavours are ripening.

Den Gyldene Freden's kavring rye loaf

4 loaves

24½ dl sifted rye flour (*råg-sikt*)
½ dl bread spices
1½ tbsp bicarb
¾ tbsp baking powder
3.75 dl black treacle
5 dl soured milk (*filmjölk*)
5 dl soured cream (*gräddfil*)

► Set the oven to 120 ºC. Run all the ingredients together in a food processor for about 2 minutes, till you have a smooth mixture. Put this into greased 1½-litre loaf tins. Bake in the bottom half of the oven for 1 hour, then raise the temperature to 150 ºC and bake for another hour. Test to see if the bread is done, and if it isn't, give it another 10–20 minutes in the oven.

Starter for rye sourdough

Day 1:
1.6 dl white flour
1.8 dl rye flour
1 dl raisins
1½ dl water
1 tsp honey
Day 3:
2.7 dl rye flour
0.8 white flour
2 dl water

► Day 1: Mix all the ingredients into a viscous batter. Cover with plastic foil and leave in a warm place at room temperature, preferably 28°C, for 2 days.

Day 3: Mix the rye flour, white flour and water into the dough from day 1. Stir and leave for another 1-2 days. The sourdough should now have a good, acidic flavour and be bubbling. The best temperature for developing sourdough is about 29°C. When the sourdough is ready for use, take what you need and store the rest in the fridge, in a lidded jar not more than half full. "Feed" the sourdough once weekly with ½ dl water and 2 tbsp white flour.

Fougasse

about 8 loaves

28⅓ dl special (professional) wheaten flour
11½ dl durum wheaten flour
1½ l water
37.5 g yeast
1½ dl olive oil
1 tbsp honey
not quite 3 tbsp salt
For working the dough:
olive oil
white flour or polenta grains

► Mix all the ingredients except the salt together in a food processor; run the machine at low speed for about 9 minutes. Add the salt and run the dough for another 3 minutes. Tip out onto a worktop and leave for 30 minutes. Divide the dough and shape it into balls weighing about 450 g each. Roll these flat and make 3 incisions in each. Brush it with olive oil and dredge in the flour or polenta grains. Transfer to a baking sheet and cover with a tea towel. Leave to rise for 1-1½ hours. Set the oven to 225 ºC. Bake for 12–15 minutes on the middle shelf.

Spicy crispbread

about 20 loaves

50 g yeast
4 dl water
1½ tbsp salt
1 pinch of crushed cloves
1 pinch of crushed ginger
1 pinch of crushed cinnamon
1 litre coarse-ground spelt flour
½ litre special wheat flour + extra for kneading the dough

► Crumble the yeast and mix it with the water. Stir till dissolved. Mix in the salt, spices and flour. Cover with a cloth and leave till doubled in size. Set the oven to 250 ºC. Divide the dough into about 20 pieces. Roll these, first with a smooth rolling pin and then with a ribbed one. Put the bread straight onto a baking tray, spray with a little water and bake in the middle of the oven for about 15 minutes. Leave it to cool on a wire rack.

Sourdough bread

about 6 loaves

Day 1:
150 g sour dough, see recipe to the left
2½ dl water
4¼ dl white flour
Day 2:
500 g of the starter
25 dl special (professional) wheaten flour
8⅓ dl pale spelt flour
1 litre water
1 tbsp honey
20 g yeast
2 tbsp salt

► Day 1: Mix the starter ingredients together in a mixing bowl. Cover with plastic foil and leave overnight at room temperature.

Day 2: Mix the starter, flour, water, honey and yeast together in a food processor. Run the machine at low speed for 9 minutes. Add the salt and run the machine for another 3 minutes. Tip out onto a floured worktop, cover with a tea towel and leave to rise for 45 minutes. Shape into loaves and place these on greased baking trays. Cover with a tea towel and leave to rise for another 1-1½ hours.

Set the oven to 250 °C. Make slits in the loaves before baking them in the lower half of the oven for 3 minutes. Now lower the oven temperature to 200 ºC and bake for another 25 minutes or so.

Sourdough rye bread with caraway

4–6 loaves

500 g rye sourdough
5 dl water
60 g yeast
½ dl honey
20 g caraway
16½ dl professional wheaten flour
4½ tsp salt

► Mix all the ingredients except the salt together in a dough mixer or food processor, running the machine at low speed for 7 minutes. Pour in the salt and mix for another 5 minutes until the dough comes away from the sides. Tip out the dough onto the worktop, cover it with a damp tea towel and leave it to rise for 1 hour. Shape it into loaves and put these in bread baskets Leave to rise for 1 hour.

Set the oven to 250 ºC. Tip out the dough into a greased baking tray. Make slits in them with a sharp knife. Put them in the lower half of the oven and throw in 2 tbsp water. Bake for 3 minutes. Lower the oven temperature to 180 ºC and bake for another 30 or 40 minutes.

Tess's mum's nut and fruit bread

4–6 loaves

2 litres soured milk (*filmjölk*)
1 tbsp bicarb
2 dl black treacle
2 dl golden syrup
18 dl Graham (coarse-ground wheaten) flour
4 dl coarse-ground rye flour
5 dl sunflower seeds
2 dl crushed linseed
2 dl hazelnuts
2 dl dried fruit, e.g. raisins, apricots or figs
4½ tbsp salt

► Set the oven to 180 ºC. Mix all the ingredients together in a large mixing bowl, preferably with a wooden spoon, until you have a smooth mixture. Transfer this to greased loaf tins of about 1½-litres capacity.

Bake in the bottom half of the oven for about 1½ hours. Remove from the oven but leave the loaves in the tins overnight to make them extra juicy.

index

Conversion table

Liquid measures
1000 ml = 1 litre
1000 ml = 10 dl
1000 ml = 100 cl

	(US)	(UK)
1 cup	= 240 ml	295 ml
	= 2.4 dl	2.95 dl
3/4 cup	= 180 ml	220 ml
	= 1.8 dl	2.2 dl
2/3 cup	= 160 ml	197 ml
	= 1.6 dl	1.97 dl
1/2 cup	= 120 ml	148 ml
	= 1.2 dl	1.48 dl
1/3 cup	= 80 ml	89 ml
	= 0.8 dl	0.89 dl
1/4 cup	= 60 ml	74 ml
	= 0.6 dl	0.74 dl

1 tbsp = 15 ml
1 tsp = 5 ml

Weight measures
1000 g = 1 kg
4 oz = 1/4 lb
      = 112 g
8 oz = 1/2 lb
      = 224 g
12 oz = 3/4 lb
      = 336 g
16 oz = 1 lb
      = 448 g
32 oz = 2 lb
      = 896 g

Length measures
1/4 inch = 0.6 cm
1/2 inch = 1.2 cm
1 inch   = 2.5 cm

Oven temperatures
122 °F = 50 °C
167 °F = 75 °C
300 °F = 150 °C
350 °F = 175 °C
392 °F = 200 °C
482 °F = 250 °C
572 °F = 300 °C

The Swedish Smörgåsbord – All the Original
Recipes in Modern Style
© Bokförlaget Max Ström
© Recipes: Gert Klötzke and Niclas Wahlström
© Texts: Donald Boström
© Photography: Per-Erik Berglund
Art Director: Donald Boström
Graphic design: Ola Svenre, jamendåså
Production: Lill Forsman and Anki Hedberg,
Bokbolaget
Recipe scrutineer: Kristina Valentin
English translation: Roger Tanner,
Ordväxlingen
Repro and printing: Fälth & Hässler,
Värnamo, 2009
Paper: Galerie Art Matt 150 g

ISBN 978-91-7126-171-7